WORDS OF LOVE

WORDS OF LOVE

A collection of winning
short stories, essays, and poems
by America's young writers

SEVEN WOLVES PUBLISHING

Library of Congress Cataloging in Publication Data

Words of Love

P.cm.

ISBN 1-56508-001-7   CIP

I. Title   MN

1 3 5 7 9 10 8 6 4 2

First Edition

Published by Frank Gargani / Seven Wolves Publishing

Edited by Laurie Holz / Seven Wolves Publishing

Spring, 1992

Quantity Purchases

Schools, companies, professional groups, clubs, and other organizations may qualify for special terms when ordering quantities of this title. For more information call 310-836-3767.

Cover design by Charles Benefiel

Contents

Acknowledgments

The publisher would like to thank the following individuals and their libraries for inspiring and informing the young people who submitted their work for this contest:

Linda Wallace and Ann Weeks of the American Library
  Association
Michelle Merrill, Beverly Hills Library
Art Dunphy, Boston Public Library
Donald Kaplan, Brooklyn Public Library
Jeri Young, Dallas Public Library
Daryl Jacobsen, Denver Public Library
Ellen Alderman, Friends of the Denver Public Library
Shauna Hawkins, Evanston (Illinois) Public Library
Andrea Lapsley, Houston Public Library
Mike Wallace, Martin Luther King Memorial Library
  (Washington, D.C.)
Jerry Peters and Bernie Bellin, Milwaukee Public Library
Nancy Liggins, Park Ridge (Illinois) Library
Mary Flourinoy, Philadelphia Public Library
Alice Meyer, Friends of the Portland Public Library
Ellen Libretto, Queens Public Library
Marcia Schneider, San Francisco Public Library
Mary Douglas, Seattle Public Library

They were also invaluable advisors and allies when it came time to arrange Michael Blake's visits in their city. And what visits they created! If ever we needed reminding that librarians are imaginative people and libraries are exciting places to be in, the enthusiasm and sheer hard work these individuals applied to this project would bring that all to mind!

We would also like to thank our wonderful judges. Each of them represents an important part of this publishing process, and each of them generously and energetically gave their time to this unique collection. We are truly honored to have had their dedication to the written word extended to these young writers and their first book.

A special acknowledgment goes to Michael Blake without whose commitment to youth and literacy this book would not have been possible.

At Seven Wolves, we were fortunate to have Abbe Beck, who manned the phones when the calls for entry forms flooded in and who spent long hours logging in and sorting the seven hundred entries. Charles Benefiel designed the book, the posters and entry forms and helped find a name for this special project. Our editor, Laurie Holz, kept us all aware of deadlines and labored to present the winners' works in their best way. Sally McCartin, our publicist, rounded up our judges, informed schools and libraries of this impending project, and gave unsparingly of her wisdom and knowledge.

And finally, a large thanks to all those terrific young people who took a chance and sent in their thoughts and dreams. Whether they find themselvs in this book or not, they are all winners, and it is to them that this book is dedicated.

Frank Gargani
Seven Wolves Publishing

"Words of Love" Judges

ELIZABETH FRANDSEN, an advertising consultant, is best known for creating "Newsroom 6," an educational television news show produced and performed by sixth graders, and a nationally recognized reading program for incarcerated juvenile offenders in California.

JAMES HOWE, award-winning author of the *Bunnicula* series, the Sebastian Barth mysteries, and other popular children's books, also writes for film and television and runs creative writing workshops for children.

SUZANNA KAPLAN, a graduate of Sarah Lawrence and the University of Pennsylvania, is a noted educator and educational consultant who resides in New York.

STEPHEN RIGGIO, executive vice president and chief operating officer of Barnes & Noble Bookstores, Inc., also serves on the New York City chapter of the Association for the Help of Retarded Children.

PATRICIA GLASS SCHUMAN, librarian, activist for free speech, and president of Neal-Schuman Publishers, also serves as president of the American Library Association.

LISA SEE, West Coast correspondent for *Publisher's Weekly*, is also a freelance writer who has co-authored three novels, including *Lotus Land*, under the pseudonym Monica Highland.

GEORGE WILLIAM SLOWIK, JR., publisher of *Publisher's Weekly*, has also served as trustee for the New York Theater Workshop, as treasurer and president of Design Industries Foundation for Aids, and is a current appointee to the Book and Library Committee of the United States Information Agency.

OREN TEICHER, associate executive director of the American Booksellers Association and president of the ABA Foundation for Free Expression, has also served as executive director of the Americans for Constitutional Freedom and as director of corporate communications for the national office of the March of Dimes.

DERRICK THOMAS, linebacker for the Kansas City chiefs and former All American, began an inner-city reading program titled "Third and Long" for which he was honored as a Library Hero.

ANN CARLSON WEEKS serves as executive director of the American Association of School Librarians and the Young Adult Library Services Association, both divisions of the American Library Association.

Introduction

Literacy and the great deeds that come with it are a must if we are going to meet the challenges of our imperiled world. Literacy is the incubator of dreams and the quality of our dreaming is going to be a crucial factor in determining the fate of our country and our planet.

As the Native Americans know so well, all things in this life are connected. I believe a life with little or no relationship to reading or writing is a life impoverished. It is a life that impoverishes the whole of our culture.

To connect with things of true and lasting value, like reading and writing, strengthens our culture. I believe that in its own small way this book restores some of the connection between young people, reading and writing and the larger world outside.

The story of how this book came to be is a good example of how positive connection can bring positive results.

The concept for this book began to take form around the publication of my second novel *Airman Mortensen*. *Airman Mortensen* concerns itself with the lives and first love of two young people and I felt from the beginning that promotion of the book should include young people in some meaningful way.

It had already been planned that I would appear at libraries nationwide. It seemed logical to invite young people from local communities to attend.

Publicist Sally McCartin took the idea a step further by

suggesting a writing contest, open to young people everywhere. Frank Gargani of Seven Wolves Publishing suggested a book be fashioned from the contest entries.

The book you hold represents positive action at work. It represents a coming together of an individual artist, a publicist and a publisher. It's a coming together of libraries and schools from all over America. It's a coming together of a distinguished panel of adult Americans who had the tough job of picking a chosen few from more than seven hundred entries.

The most important connection made in this book is with the young writers themselves, the young writers whom those of us directly involved are so proud to encourage.

The work of these young writers demonstrates unique skill and perception. It exemplifies the undying nature of hope we all have for our country. Above all, this beautiful work proves that the spirit of love is still alive in our world.

Michael Blake
Tucson, Arizona
April, 1992

WORDS OF LOVE

VELVET PETALS
by Bethany E. Gradert, *Geneseo, Illinois*

Velvet petals scattered on the warm
pavement, a crimson carpet moist
with tears; he loves me not.

LOVE IS NOT

by James Burlingame, *Oakland, California*

Love is not hope. Love is not the sun, love is not the stars. Love is not the action, the thought, or the word. Love is neither here nor there. Love is neither pleasure nor pain, truth nor deceit. Love is no simile at all.

Love is but an emotion created by man's need to co-exist with himself; love is but a reason for things to happen — a consent to kiss and kill. Love holds no surprise, no innocence. Love has been and will be many times. Love is a sociological adaptation, yet another survival defense created by the first animal to unlearn its natural instincts. Love is as natural as the tomahawk.

Love is here to get you there and all other definitions are beautiful untruths, existing solely to compensate for the guilt you feel when questioning the balance of the transaction taking place. Love is a lie no one questions, everyone believes — a truth so accepted that its real purpose is ignored and unknown. So enjoyed, so sacred that to question the validity of its assumed form of existence is to commit perjury of the highest kind.

To insult the beliefs and comforts of mankind, so assigned by the evolution of society, would be to strip the world of its symbols and scapegoats, leaving it open to its inextricable conscience — something which stirs ominously even at the thought of such a trial. To do so would be suicide. Love is the last shield; the smile, the handshake covering the intent.

THE DEATH OF BRITTA ANN

by Louisa Bennion, *Spring City, Utah*

My sister Zina and I knew all about butchering. Many times we had seen it done, sitting on the pigsty rails with the butcher's boy, laughing and trying to push each other off into the reeking, trompled pig-mud and blood. Of course Zina and I never watched the actual killing, but as soon as we heard the shot we would dash out of the house to watch the fat butcher in his splattered apron and bloody bare hands and his rubber boots that made obscene noises in the muck. He would hang the pig on the crane on the back of his truck, and then skin it with quick, expert strokes of his knife. He would tell us the name of every steaming organ that came out, and we would laugh in surprise when the shining white fat of the naked pig would quiver and twitch as the nerves settled into death.

But those pigs were really just pigs. My father would buy them as weanlings and we would give them funny names like Tammy Faye Bacon. But Zi and I knew that they would die and we would eat them in the fall, and we were expert at becoming fond of them, yet holding part of ourselves away from them so that when fall came we wouldn't be attached to them and grieve their passings. But Britta Ann was different. We watched as she was born and named her after a good friend. We raised her from a sweet-smelling black piglet with a white band around her belly to a huge and gentle sow with stiff hair on her back and a not entirely unpleasant musky smell. She wasn't butchered, but kept as a brood sow, so my sister and I knew it was safe to give ourselves to her in open love. She was nearly as human as we were, it seemed. She had her own little wooden shack with a tin roof and bright lamps to keep her babies warm. Every day she would sweep her house out with her snout, for she hated dust and messiness. She even pooped in a far corner of her pen, never near her house. But if she wanted a mud bath, she knew how to turn on the water pump. My father was her favorite person, and she would welcome him with high-pitched grunts of delight whenever he came bearing a bucket of slops. And when she was truly happy and at peace with the world, with her trough full of grain and slime, her tightly curled tail would go limp, and she would mutter happy things to herself as she ate.

One spring after Britta had her babies, she got very sick. She lost her milk and we had to give the piglets away. The vet said that Britta would probably die if she gave birth again. When fall came my parents decided that Britta would have to go — she served no practical use now and was far too expensive to keep as a pet.

When the day came, grey and dismal, Zina and I didn't play on the fence with the butcher's boy. We huddled on Zi's bed, remembering Britta's golden life and peering out the window to see her cheerfully eating her last meal. The butcher was setting things ready, his face blank of emotions despite the horrible thing he was going to do. His boy was sloshing restlessly about in the mud and flinging pebbles at the rain barrel. After all, this was just another of the countless fat pigs.

I shuddered when I heard the close shot; it slammed into me with the truth that Britta was really dead, forever gone, beyond any rescue. I wondered why she'd ever lived at all.

My mother came and found us a few minutes later. I looked into her face and began to sob.

"I'm never, ever going to eat Britta Ann!" I cried bitterly, "You can't make me!"

But I let my mother fold her long arms around me and hold me. I saw that the edges of her eyes were red. Her voice wavered as she spoke, "How do you think Britta would feel if she could hear you?"

I pondered this, wondering whose side Mom was on. I knew that Britta's death wasn't really my mother's fault, and I felt a twinge of guilt for having blamed her and Dad so harshly in my mind. But wouldn't I be sticking up for Britta if I didn't eat her?

"She led the best life a pig could," my mother went on, hugging Zi and I to her, "she lived in the sun and had plenty of good, fresh food. She got to raise several litters of babies. If you eat a pig from the store, it most likely lived in misery in a tiny pen with lots of other pigs who get fed chemicals and boring mash. And Britta died happily. When the butcher came into her pen with his gun, she stopped eating and went right up to meet him. It must have been hard on him to pull the trigger. But when she died, her tail was limp.

"She bears us no hard feelings. I'm sure she knows that we needed the meat and couldn't afford to feed her through the winter. She just wants to thank us for being so good to her. If you don't eat Britta, her death will have been in vain."

My mother groped for a Kleenex. But Zina and I just buried our streaming faces in her.

Britta's meat was delicious, more tender than any pork I've ever tasted. That was years ago, though, and we have long since eaten the last of Britta. But the memory of her love is still with me, and I've never seen the eating of meat in the same taken-for-granted way. Thank you, Britta Ann.

UNREQUITED
by Heather L. Firth, *Raleigh, North Carolina*

Among the lofty clouds stands yonder tree,
a handsome fellow, strong and stately made,
but in his beauty solitary is he,
save one small sprout that growest in his shade.
When bitter winds blow 'cross the barren fields,
still warm and sweet the sap flows in his veins,
to dream of love that such contentment yields
which ends his loneliness and heals his pains.
While far below the sapling in her spot
dost gaze in yearning at the tree above,
but for her tender youth he seest her not,
nor knowst the silent passions of her love.
So I the sprout and thou the lonely tree,
who knowest not the love I hold for thee.

FARAWAY BROWN EYES

by Jason Norment, *Houston, Texas*

Last night I went out...with a girl
                         with faraway brown eyes.

And we spoke of: clubs, siblings, and how waiters only
        ask you if everything is fine
            when you have food in your mouth.

And as we ate our dinner, we drank in silence and
        laughter.
                        (She would not look at me,
                            but instead, stared into space)
(Occasionally I caught her glance
    and saw a mysterious world...)

I took her to a park, but it was wet and cold,
so we sat in the car, and played the lovers' game of Mind.
I could not tell what I was doing, I would not let myself
        know...
    But we sat in silence and I bathed in her warm glow.
She was like nothing I've experienced before. As I sat in the
    car, I wanted her more. And yet, we did not exist.
        (I could only catch glimpses of her beautiful eyes.)

I taught her to look at me, and she did look into me, and we
  played the lovers' game of Mind...because we did not exist.
She would look into me and I would look into her
                      (but we did not exist)
and we would play the lovers' game of Mind
  (I was afraid to touch her   (She was not
      I did not want   used to touching
        to hurt her.)   but she would be touched.)

When I touched her, her eyelids fell over her eyes, basking in
  touch. (My fingers tingled.)
        (Her smile faded.)

We played a new game, while she basked in touch and I
    bathed in beauty;
      while I watched her face and her eyelids.

One step at a time in this slow ritual ( ) led to another.
  But time bends so slowly,...and we, so artfully, until
    the last
  drink was sapped...   (carefully)

              ...and savored.

Eventually we surfaced our world for air,
              She opened her eyes,
                    and we sat...
                      ...in silence.

Jason Norment

And then she told me to close my eyes,
     darkness descended upon my me,
       and she kissed me.
(Ever so gently)
  (My lips tingled)
    (My mind swam) — I asked her why
      she asked me to close my eyes; she said
      she was afraid I would say no.

Then she asked — if I would've kissed her; I said no,
        but only because
(I did not want to hurt her.)
      Then I kissed her.

Yes, I kissed her.

And she trembled, and told me and told me not to be afraid,
And as she said this, she placed my hand my hand on her
heart...( )

I marveled at how I could touch her,
     and she could kiss me,
      and although it moved me,
how it was (not) sexual—
     how it did not feel sexual,
How we kissed   and yet, did not
How I touched her   and yet, did not
How I felt about her   ( )

Now I wander around in this new world
      that has no corners, and bump into everything
In a daze,
        eyes aglaze,
            not existing.
            I think I must have stripped
              the corners from this world, so I
              would not be hurt again. . .

I LOVE HENRY

by Hollie Scott, *Denver, Colorado*

I love Henry, my $15, pseudo crushed velvet, 1950's made, oil stained, green-gold, squeaky, eye-sore of a recliner that sits snugly in the northwest corner of my room. I affectionately refer to him as my ''death chair'' because ten minutes in his warm embrace is enough to put you in dreamland— not because one look at him is enough to put you six feet under.

Mind you, this is no ordinary ugly recliner. This chair, my chair, has an easy going temperament. Henry will sit in that drafty corner for hours without a single complaint, never will pick a fight, always listens, and never, ever interrupts. I suppose that's why I love him so much. It's comforting to know that there's a pair of soft, fuzzy arms longing to greet me after a trying day out and about. He never asks where I've been, or what time I came home. Henry is a much better friend than my cat, Smoker, because I don't have a litter box to look after and he never needs to be fed.

Henry is shaped like an average straight-backed, regal, out of date swivel recliner, made comfortable after years of carefree use in front of the television. He has had only one owner so it's been difficult for him to adjust to me, but I think that the transition has been smooth up to this point. Some people just don't understand the heartache involved in such a case.

No matter how my Henry looks on the outside, I will

love him until he is nothing more than just scraps of fuzz. My Henry is one of a kind. He is nothing like a brand new Lazy-Boy; hours of precious time were spent breaking him in. Henry's a bit dirty, but at least he's comfortable. I will never have to wait for him to hit his prime years — Henry's already there. Though Henry is an eyesore, his beauty lies underneath all that tacky upholstry where the Kevin Costner of recliners is hiding. He's quite handsome when accented with a blanket (preferably one without holes). There's not too many men who improve with a throw cover, and fewer who would allow you to "bag" them.

Finally...Henry accepts me. He doesn't accept me for my true inner self; after all, he is a recliner. Henry does accept me with my ratty hair, smeared lipstick, cranky disposition— some of my better qualities I display before noontime. He'll never complain if I haven't showered, a favorite pasttime I have often suggested to him. I will never have to impress him with my looks, because frankly he doesn't impress me. All we need are each other's comforting arms. I love being in love with my $15, pseudo crushed velvet, oil stained, green-gold, squeaky eyesore of a recliner that sits snugly in the northwest corner of my room.

LOVE IS LIKE A SEASHELL
by Andrew Blair, *New Bern, North Carolina*

Love is like a seashell
sometimes floating free and other times you're all
    washed up
Love is like a nomad
staying where it prospers most
Love is like a black hole
taking you to a point of no return
Love is like a wild ride
to some it's great and to others it's sickening
Love is like a tomato
easy to grow, easy to squash
Love is like a dumb school rule
nobody understands it
Love is like a bad ending
it changes your idea about it.

U.P.S.

by Nicole Krauss, *Old Westbury, New York*

The afternoon sun cast a gentle glow about the room, darting behind the leaves of the avocado plants and dahlia flowers that she tended. When she bought the dahlia she didn't know that it symbolized instability; she probably wouldn't have chosen it at the nursery had she known. But she hadn't, and it didn't seem to matter much now anyway.

The sun was a perfect match for the early spring wind that tossed the new leaves outside. The kitchen was warm and comfortable, and lounging at the table, she pushed thoughts of the dust and debris that she had examined this morning behind the washing machine from her mind. She was actually looking for a sock to complete a pair, but instead she found dust and debris: a clear sign of untidiness, she had once read in a magazine. But that didn't seem to matter much now anyway.

The catalogue she was browsing through wasn't particularly interesting. Some items caught her eye, and she circled them with a yellow marker: "the isometric toner for women. Curve-Shaper is an isometric, low-impact, muscle-toning device that uses resistence and repetition to tone and shape your body." She finished her coffee, closed the magazine and put it on top of the refrigerator.

Her husband never noticed the plethora of mail order items that lined the shelves and tables and filled the closets

Nicole Krauss

of the house. Or maybe he just never mentioned it. It was
hard to tell if he noticed anything. But the hall closet was
filled with tricky, mechanical Hammacher Schlemmer items,
and the white chest in the bedroom was lined with cruise
clothes from Spiegal for vacations that they never took.

She always watched from the kitchen while he sat in
the den opening the credit-card bills at the end of the month.
She listened for her name that he never called, an angry shout
that she never heard, a flash of annoyance across his face
which she never saw. It was almost a game that she always
lost, but he might not have known that he was playing.

She couldn't remember if something was due today or
not. If she ordered it on Saturday, then it would come tomor-
row, because it usually took five work days. If she called on
Sunday, though, it would probably arrive today. She couldn't
remember if she had decided on the Orthopedic Pet Bed or
the Traditional Chinese Accupressure Balls. She didn't
actually believe in accupressure, so she probably ordered the
pet bed.

She went in the bathroom to put on some make-up
anyway. Her hair was a thin mousy color that fell unevenly
around her cheeks, giving her an almost childish look. Light
freckles left over from her childhood covered her nose. She
painted her lips with a dark red color and brushed her thin
hair into place. She pursed her freshly glossed lips in the
mirror and, leaving the tube of lipstick uncapped, she left
the bathroom and walked down the hall, swinging her hips
smoothly. In her bedroom she put on a flowered button-

down shirt. She glanced in the mirror, and smiled. She never put on lipstick for her husband.

The doorbell rang while she was watering the avocado plant.

"Hello, Ma'am," he said in his Southern drawl.

She saw the U.P.S. man every week and he still called her "Ma'am." She always took the package first and signed her name. Then she invited him inside, just like she had the first time. A slight sweat had gathered on his brow, maybe from the afternoon sun, maybe from her perfume; she couldn't tell.

He sat nervously on the piano bench, the closest seat to the door. She offered him a cold drink, as if she had no clue what would happen next. She enjoyed the power, the control as he watched her every move.

"No, Ma'am, I'm not thirsty," was the polite, mechanical reply. He couldn't have been more than twenty-five. She circled him as he stared straight ahead, and then sat down next to him and played with the buttons on his brown uniform as he sat stiffly on the bench. She turned his cheek and kissed him hard on the lips.

He knew what came next, and soon they were on the floor half-naked, his uniform bunched around his ankles. After a while, she pushed him away, and ordered him to get dressed, which he did quickly, his face red. She waited, leaning against the wall. As he struggled with the brown buttons, she walked to the door, motioned him out, and closed it behind him. She took the catalogue off the refrigerator and tried to decide between the Curve Shaper and the Infravib Massage.

Her husband came home at 6:45, and they didn't talk much at dinner. He didn't comment on the new place mats she had ordered, so she didn't ask him about work. He was going bald and it didn't suit him whatsoever. She cleared the table and he turned on the news. He always put it on loud, louder than anything else he watched, almost as if the volume would make it all the more serious. She stretched the phone into the kitchen.

"Yes, I'd like to order something." They always asked for your credit card number first, as if you would order something, laugh hysterically and then hang up.

"Item number A1076. The Curve Shaper. Yes, I want it shipped to the address on the catalogue. No, that's all. You're welcome." She hung up, and left the phone where it was, its cord stretched between the den and the kitchen.

"Two people shot on the subway in the city," he said to whoever was listening, namely no one. She couldn't understand why anyone would want to watch the news. It was asking for depression and sad stories, neither of which she wanted. It was early, but she climbed the stairs to the bedroom.

"I want to talk to you this time, O.K.?" she asked the boy.

"Sure, Ma'am," he responded nervously. He answered

her questions with three-word answers, never looking at her, always staring straight ahead. He was twenty-six and never went to college. This is hopeless, she thought. The red name inscribed on his uniform said "JIM." She had never noticed that before. She didn't particularly love the name "Jim".

She circled him, and his brow began to sweat. This time it definitely wasn't from the afternoon sun. She touched his shoulders and he flinched. She kissed his ear, and then his mouth. He smelled like the outdoors, of pine trees. He was breathing heavily, and she thought she heard him whisper "Ma'am" softly. She enjoyed exciting him, she enjoyed controlling him.

"You can kiss me back. I don't want to talk any more."

He did, softly first. He stayed for an hour, and soon she pushed him away. He dressed quickly in front of the dahlia plant. She wanted to giggle at his clumsiness, his jagged movements. But she didn't, and only after she shut the door behind him did she smile.

She ripped open the brown packaging that the order was cased in. The Curve Shaper was not blue like they had advertised in the catalogue, but rather a muted yellow, faintly reminiscent of unseasoned bananas. She turned it over, held it in front of her, and examined it carefully. It was basically a horseshoe-shaped, flexible plastic piece with springs. It was silly looking and she left it lying dejectedly on the coffee table with the shredded packaging. She would try it out tomorrow.

She remembered when her husband used to tell her that

she was beautiful. They would lie together for hours, him whispering gently to her from time to time. She felt beautiful too, and everything was fresh and young; there was no debris behind the washing machine, and the dahlia plants were tiny buds. But sometime, she didn't exactly know when, it had changed; their hair grew thin, and everything grew old and tired. Sometimes, reclining in the brown easy chair in the den, she would imagine what her husband would say if he caught her with the U.P.S. man. She could picture his eyes widening and his puckered mouth open. She smiled.

On Friday, with her lips painted red, and streaks of blue visible on her eyelids, she answered the door. A man in a brown suit with U.P.S. scrawled in place of the name stood before her, offering her the brown, sealed package. She stared at his grey hair and flannel fisher hat. His face was covered with a black stubble. He opened his mouth to speak, and she slammed the door in his face. As she ran upstairs, she heard him shouting ''Yo, lady! Lady, I got a damn package for you!'' She buried her face in the pillows and held her breath until she heard the truck drive away.

She felt betrayed. Maybe Jim wasn't excited by her after all. She felt old and grey, although her hair was still all the same mousy color. She sat in the brown armchair and made up stories of how he was kidnapped, and all he kept saying to the bandits was ''I need to make a delivery...'' Her delivery, of course.

The next week, as she filled the watering can, the faucet

began spurting water everywhere. She grabbed a towel and helplessly threw it over the sink. She ran into the living room and searched under all the stacks of books for the Yellow Pages. She could hear the water spraying in the kitchen. She threw open the closet and began to hurl things off the shelves in search of the Nynex. Finally, she found it under some plastic file cabinets that she had never used.

"P...Pl...Plumber," she ran her fingers up and down the pages, and finally, almost in utter despair, she found one nearby. She grabbed the yellow marker lying on the end table and hurriedly circled the name. She dialed the number in such a hurry that she pressed a wrong digit and had to hang up and dial again. The water filled the sink and began sliding onto the floor. She watched it helplessly, ignoring even the dahlias which were about to be flooded. Finally, the doorbell rang. She ran and opened it up. A man in a blue suit and a tool box stood awkwardly at the door. He was young, maybe twenty-eight.

"Come in," she said.

ME

by Angie Phelps, *Monpelier, Idaho*

Some people want to go to the moon,
me, I want to get out of the house.
Some people want to write a novel,
me, I don't want to write at all.
Some people want to read *Gone With The Wind,*
me, I want to read *Curious George.*
Some people want to learn to sing,
me, I want to sing off key.
Some people want to be in style,
me, I want to be comfortable.
Some people want a real cute "friend",
me, I want someone who's nice.
Some people want to watch the fight,
me, I want to be in it.
Some people want to listen to what's being said,
me, I want to say it.
Some people want a nice, fast car,
me, I want something that runs.
Some people want to stay awake all night,
me, I want to go to sleep.
Some people want to frown all the time,
me, I want to smile some too.
Some people want to go through life,
me, I want to live it.
Some people want to take their time,

me, I want to get where I'm going.
Some people want to be something they're not,
me, I just want to be ME

WAITING BEHIND A WALL FOR A SHOOTING STAR
by Emily Luce, *San Francisco, California*

I cannot help
remembering
when you kissed me.
And where and how.
Every once in a while
something of it
comes back to me—
how I was so completely
conscious
of your hand on my back...
my eyes were closed
but I could see everything.
My stomach flips
and I almost shiver
and I have to control the urge
to smile.

UNSPOKEN LOVE
by Quang Ngo, *Stafford, Texas*

Night guards the city from event. Across the opal miles silence calls. The stars twinkle upon the firmament a foreign language, as if they plan a fate — for heaven or for hell. Life awes me. I sit. I wish Pa is here with me and we enjoy the cool together. I love Pa. He died in the Viet Nam War when I was thirteen and small at heart and young at mind. I love Pa, but a Communist soldier said "This man's no good."

In August 1967, we moved into the countryside a thousand kilometers from Qui Ngon. Pa built a small house from bamboo trees, cocoanut leaves, and red earth, and there we lived. At dawn before the first indication of day, Pa and I rose. In the small, cold kitchen dimly lit by a kerosene lamp, we savored the thin rice soup and listened to the wind outside. Then Pa placed a mighty hoe upon his shoulder and I followed him west because I was a man. We traveled seven kilometers on bare foot to our land in the forest. This we did each day. Once, a water snake bit my left leg, and I cried like a child. Pa put some bitter herbs on the wound and cradled me home. But the Communist soldier said "This man's no good."

During the winter of 1968, the land froze like glaciers atop Mount Everest. We stayed home. We labored hard the months before; fortune blessed us with a handsome harvest. We filled two grain bins and still had several small bags extra. One morning as Pa was mending the clay bowl and I was whetting the dull blades, drumbeats as if from Erebus stirred the frigid silence and cracked the dagger-like crystals on the roof. Pa looked out the window and saw a train of peasants in black from Mr. Chin's house nearby. Hung, the old man's precious son, had died of appendicitis.

When winter passed and we again combed the field, Mr. Chin grew ill from grief. He could not toss the land, so Pa gave him grain. When Mr. Chin coughed fire, Pa fed him medicine. When Mr. Chin recovered and offered his service, Pa only smiled and cooked him supper. But the Communist soldier said "This man's no good."

A hundred paces to the left of our house a river ran from the Indian Ocean. The waterway provided a major transportation system for the small village and served as an important resource. In the spring when the rain god drew forth shower, the river flowed with richness. But in the summer months the riverbed dried. The officials of the town ordered the men to dig the river deeper so water would run. Pa would carry his shovel to the bank and work. When night came, he wiped off the earnest sweat, and said "If we continue this for two more days, the river will run again." But the Communist soldier said "This man's no good."

In October 1972, after Pa harvested the cornfield, the local official called him to war. The country shook with powerful bombs and men died each day. But Pa was not afraid, and when he marched off for the country, neither did his hands tremble nor did his eyes give tears. He told me

"Watch the land until I come back." And he walked away. Twice he wrote from camp and said nothing of the war. By the end of January, Pa fell upon the earth. And so I did not weep. But the Communist soldier said "This man's no good."

I COME FROM WHERE THE WIND BEGINS

by Joseph Obezo, *Flagstaff, Arizona*

I come from where the wind begins
last of a dying race
I come from where the wind begins
please look into my face

Can you see the snow capped mountains
can you see the sun-bleached sands,
can you see the dead remains
of once beautiful land

Oh how the oaks and willow trees
dug deep into the earth
swaying gently in the breeze
while Father Time showed his mirth

I come from where the wind begins
last of a dying race
I come from where the wind begins
my home that's been erased

Oh I can see the morning sun
upon the Eastern clouds
and I can see the midnight fog
dressed in ghostly shrouds

I COME FROM WHERE THE WIND BEGINS

I can see the blooming flowers,
feel the ancient breeze,
see the rolling knolls and hills
I could wander where I pleased

I come from where the wind begins
last of a dying race
I come from where the wind begins
remembering a forgotten place

VICTOR AND PRISCILLA
by Mark A. Gede, *Dover, Delaware*

"TEN." Today is quite peaceful. The tropic sun on my face. The birds, the breeze, the fragrances. A full belly. God, I love life!...This place is really remote. Never envisioned that eight years of college, a Ph.D., thousands of hours in a lab would lead me to this corner of the world.

"NINE." Priscilla was in a good mood the last time we talked. Don't really know why, especially with all that's been going on. My late hours in the lab, my coming home stressed out and cranky. I'm glad I'm finally getting this over. God, I hope everything goes all right.

"EIGHT." That guy has a grizzly voice. The way he intones the countdown chills my soul...I hope the hummingbirds got enough nectar this morning. The sugar water solution I suggested to Prill should satisfy them. I couldn't bear thinking they might go hungry. They've become so dependent on us...The dog seems to enjoy his new food. That ear infection he has is really puzzling...

"SEVEN." Pshew, this place is getting hot. No tropic fragrances in here! Wish I could go outside and get a breath of fresh air...I'm really looking forward to that long walk I've promised Prill when I get back home. Yosemite is at its grandest this time of year. I'm glad Prill and I made the big move to the park. God has to have caressed every square centimeter of his world there.

"SIX." I really thought my years at Princeton would get me into something other than this. Hoped I could be creating useful energy. I'm glad people are beginning to accept nuclear power more readily. But it still scares me; it's not quite under control...God, I hope I'm doing the right thing.

"FIVE." This room's becoming quite sticky. I hope I got enough insulin this morning. I was in such a hurry. Wish I'd gotten a better breakfast, too. I'm getting hungry. Or is it nervousness that's rattling me?...I've worked so long. I hope everything goes all right. God, I hope this is the right thing...

FOUR." America. What a beautiful country! How I love it! All my years of work have been for it only...Gonna' spend more time with my wife. Wonder what that noise was. Seems the breeze is picking up.

"THREE." Boy it's barren out there. How could plants live here? Why would they want to? You know, nuclear physics isn't all bad. But I'm so glad my daughter's a park ranger. "Dr. Gede, you all set?" Boy, he's...

"TWO." ...really young to be working here. But all that matters is the experience. All my hours studying, all my hours teaching have not prepared me for this. No professor ever suggested to me how to calm the butterflies in my stomach. No mentor ever hinted this would ever play so much havoc with my conscience.

"ONE." That is it! Please let me have done the right thing! I really love my family; I truly love all nature. I need

to write about this...There it is!...God, that's awesome.
The power...My guilt is as heavy as the fallout. What have
I done?...

On that morning in 1948, on the Enewetak Atoll in the
Marshall Islands, Victor Philip Gede witnessed the detona-
tion of his nuclear test bomb "Priscilla", named for his wife.

THOUGHTS OF A CHILD-BEARING CHILD

by Elizabeth Adler, *Santa Barbara, California*

People.
They come. They stay. They go.
Passing through your life as a dream passes through
your mind and whispers out the cracks in the windows
leaving a pale frost in the night. Leaving only a memory,
and nothing more.
Except perhaps
a faint hint of love that's remembered
because of the blossoms left to die in the vase.
It was love wasn't it?
Was it a storm or was it only a summer's breeze?
Did it hit me or did it only brush gently against
my hand? To tell you the truth
I can't remember. It seems like an eternity ago.
It could have been yesterday; maybe it's tomorrow.
At the time it raged intensely like a fire
out of control and like the forked tongue of flames,
it lashed out and burned me
When the fire went out, I was left with a scar.
        I wear it now
as Hester Prynne wore her scarlet letter;
        for all to see and all to evaluate.
But unlike her, I have not learned from my sin
and I have compounded it, for with two

Elizabeth Adler

we have given life and breath to a third.
My punishments have been unspeakable and eternally
they will burden me while I continue
to burden those whom I have betrayed.
The struggle will be long and perhaps
I will collapse with exhaustion. All I can do
is hope for the future, hope for a memory and
nothing more.

FROM WHERE I STAND

by Nicole Krauss, *Old Westbury, New York*

Through the labyrinth of my life you follow me, running and hiding in my sidelong shadow. You can keep up with my quickstep, for it is from you that I got my hurried walk. In the beginning, during that first gray November, I would suddenly freeze and whip around, expecting to see you standing there, silk scarf wrapped around your neck, beige pumps caught in a step. I quickly learned, however, that I would never quite be able to see you or touch you. Still, you are always there, rocking in the chair beside my bed as I sleep, clapping in the last row of the theater, tripping the people who try to hurt me. I feel you even now, leaning over my shoulder, squinting at the words, reaching into your heavy bag for your magnifying glasses.

The last time I saw you was in 1972, in New York. We were in a yellow taxi cab, and you were late as usual. In your thick Russian accent, you called to the driver to let you out. It was in front of Rockefeller Center, and the giant tree glistened and sparkled with tiny flashing lights. When you kissed my cheek, I inhaled the strong smell of perfumed elegance on your skin mixed with the soft mustiness of your fur coat. As the cab pulled away, I saw your thick ankles sliding quickly into the thick crowd.

When it happened, no one really wanted to discuss details. We used the certain words that one uses when something tragic happens. We spoke in low tones and we each grieved alone, in our secret places. At the very end, after the accident, after the month of hospital smells and sterility, at the very end when we knew it was all over, we cried together, heaving into each other's arms, shaking and trembling through the night. There was an emptiness inside of us and the silence seemed heavier, our favorite colors seemed drab.

We went through your things — the racks of linen skirts and silk blouses, the stacked boxes of scarves, the lines of solid pumps. I didn't want anything. In the same hushed hospital tones they had been using for a month, they whispered that I was not taking it well. They left me alone, and I sat in the middle of the closet, my head inside the hem of the hanging fur coat. A gold engraved perfume pot on the dresser sparkled in the dim light. It fit into my dry and cracked palm, glowing delicately in my clumsy hand. Opening the lid, it suddenly felt as if you were next to me, that close; I could smell you. I put the pot in my pocket and closed the closet doors behind me.

Walking toward the elevator, I heard the quick clicking of heels on the marble floor behind me. The man who shoved me to the side as he got out of the elevator tripped and fell on his nose. When I stepped out into the sunshine, it felt new and warm on my face.

You have somehow found the place in my life you always wanted — a permanent pillar of strength supporting me, holding me straight. You cackle tremendously at the jokes I make that no one else thinks are funny; you blow raspberries at the critics when they rip my plays to shreds. In your linen skirts and beige pumps you stand on the last seat in the last row, whistling, screaming, and clapping whenever I enter the spotlight for a final bow.

I see your face on that day in November of 1972 clearly now. Your eyes were sparkling when you said goodbye. Thinking of it now, it was as if you knew you weren't really going anywhere at all.

I SAW A YOUNG GIRL
by Molly Crawford, *New Bern, North Carolina*

I saw a young girl
so full of young love
picking daisy blossoms
by the crystal blue pond.

I saw a young bride
all dressed in white
in love with a young man.
I heard her sing
of true love
And I watched her pick daisies
in the yellow sun.

I saw an old woman
rocking on a porch
with her old husband.
They did not speak
they only watched
the daisies grow.

Headline:
LIGHTNING STRIKES TWICE
by Kristin Putchinski, *Plano, Texas*

She stands — her hands whitened by her death grip on the umbrella — in front of the lonely grave. Lightning strikes a mile away: she does not flinch at the sound. Only stands — solemn, abysmal. Normally, she would talk to him, but she is held back by the thought of the holiday travelers. Their eyes glued to her — rudely curious — invading her privacy ...but what is private about a cemetery?

She does begin to talk: telling him about her chemistry test that day. How she couldn't get her locker open before third period. How she felt the tears, like acid, burning her cheeks when she found a bill in the mail addressed to him.

But she is not crying now. There is no pressure from school, no homework to worry about — the teachers understanding about "family trips" over the holiday.

Oh, how the word "family" had pierced her heart. Like a dagger, rusted and twisting, severing nerves that supplied the heart. The fear of the knife makes her tired and restless.

She drops the umbrella, looks to the sky, and welcomes the raindrops on her face. She opens her mouth to scream — not caring that the people on the highway might see her; not caring that her clothes and her hair are soaked...were they not soaked earlier by the blood of her own heart?

Yes, they were, she answers.

"Yes," she says aloud.

Now, screaming into the rain,
>to the people on the road,
>to the grave at her feet: "YES!"

She glances at the ground that, from the day of her loss has left questions unanswered: ...Why?...

She kneels and puts her ear to the ground . . . a heartbeat.

Faint, but unmistakable.

Her eyes fill with longing, but it subsides as she realizes it is her own heart that pounds in her ears.

She is cold now, shivering.

It is time to go home.

Still kneeling, her knees covered in mud, she places her head once more to the ground and whispers: "Yes...I do miss you."

And she does not move as lightning strikes a mile away.

EL AMOR ESTA UNA MENTIROZA

by Andrea Ohlson, *Lacey, Washington*

Love lies. Love creates confusion. I know this because I've watched it at work and I've spoken to it. I've breathed it and lived alongside it. I've touched it and yearned with the beauty of it, and I've felt it die. I've felt love bury itself in the ashes and remains of a fire it once kindled. I've felt love hide itself in night's shadows and fade before the morning's light could betray it. I know why love lies; so I've grown tired of being part of it. Sometimes it returns softly, tiptoeing behind me. It whispers cunningly through me , but I have locked it out and I am safe. Love lies. Love betrays.

I once wanted to know love's scent of old leather and harsh soap. I hoped to feel it reaching through me, enfolding me in silken arms. But love pulled me from my hiding places with hands of ice. It stole my securities and escaped with the person I once was. So, with the scattered stones of my life, I have built a smooth, impenetrable wall. Love's prying fingers won't locate any cracks to reach through or ledges to climb upon.

Love tortures and haunts those who pursue it after it has gone. It leaves behind but memories, recalling tastes of angry words and bitter agony. Its fragrance is a sour musk. Memories of love are tired and silent and worn. Memories want only to learn from love's passing and to forget what remains. But I have not forgotten the pain which remains

Andrea Ohlson

and I am wise to love. It cannot leave within me its promises and memories and disillusions.

Love is hungry. Love stretches over aching days and holds with arms of false tranquility.

Love is cruel, but love does not discriminate. The poor, the rich, the angry, the meek, the old; they have known love. They have been tricked by love. I know because I've witnessed love at play. Love lies to those who believe their fantasies. I know. My mother married my father in love. My mother planned to finish her college education and get a degree in social sciences. My father wanted to be a teacher. But he found a job with the state, supposing it would be a better income. My mother stayed home to raise my brother and me. Love left them nothing but failed dreams of hope, filthy from overuse. Love changed while they turned their backs to raise a family and love disappeared. Love escaped with the trouble and the heartaches. Love fled while my mother changed the diapers, and as my father worked figures behind a large gray desk stuffed in an orange cubicle. As it fled, love revealed the follies in their lives and their shoddy achievements. Love left my father bitter and hateful, and left my mother broken.

I despise love. I know why it lies and why it betrays. It lied to me because I wanted it to, and it betrayed me when I let it become my master. Love is tangible as smoke and transparent as time. If love is nurtured it becomes leather; soft and comfortable and warm. If ignored, it becomes the choking dark green leaves of a forgotten weed. I did not intentionally ignore love. The weed seemed a flower, growing without need of care or tending. Love deceives.

Love is not my master any longer. Love's lies cannot lead me to the cliffs of desperate, reaching hope and crashing, aching wrenching despair. I am scared and I am empty, but I am free and I am wise to love.

But as love cannot reach me, neither can joy and longing, and passion and fury. Without love, emotion finds no place in me. So I rest...waiting.

I MUST MOVE ON
by Pedro Hernandez, Jr., *Dallas, Texas*

I'm not ready for true love.
I need to explore my world first.
I'm young and need to grow
and find the perfect girl.

I'm sorry that I hurt you,
but it's time that I move on.
Your tears of pain I wipe away
as you cry to our love song.

I didn't mean to hurt you,
I'm sorry I made you cry.
I thought that you would understand
I'm a bird that needs to fly.

I'm never going to forget you —
you're special in my life.
I'll be loving you always
when I rest and when I die.

I know that I'm a part of you
and your heart is filled with me.
Maybe one day you'll realize
why this was meant to be.

I know I'm not explaining myself,
but I hope you understand.
Maybe in the future
we'll reach and rejoin our hands.

'Til then. . .I love you.

HE TOOK HIS TROUBLES

by Heathre Maree Schmitz, *Algoma, Wisconsin*

He took his troubles and sorrows and made them into pebbles. He lay them at his feet with the biggest and heaviest at the bottom. Slowly the pile grew into a wall that blocked out life. She came along and removed a pebble, allowing a little bit of life to shine in. He realized what she had done for him and began to take the smallest pebbles and hand them to her. Instead of becoming weighed down and tossing them aside, like he thought she might, she began to construct a bridge. Carefully and meticulously she placed each pebble so that one day he could walk from the cold, dark place his world had become, into the world of light and freedom she had created with love and compassion.

PHOEBE AND ME
by Michael Bird, *Hingham, Massachusetts*

Novem ber 7

Phoebe explained to me today that every snow flake is the same. Wow. There are so many snow flakes I can't believe they are all the same! She's so smart. It's almost lunch.

November 8

I love Phoebe. She's beautiful and left handed. She said I am left handed too. Maybe I'll kis her. I hope tomorrow! Until then I will look at her and she will talk to me and tell me more stories.

November 9

Phoebe's sick but I'm not. She wouldn't talk all day to me. Her cheeks aren't red like usual and she's not smiling or talking in her sleep like usual. She's probably sleeping. My food is here.

November 10

The doctors said Phoebe will get better soon. Good! Maybe when they take us outside I'll kis her near the fountain on the grass. She swore at the nurse today. I love her anyway.

November 11

Phoebe said that if you hang an orchestra from the ceiling the coosticks will be better. I don't know what she's talking about. The doctors said they were proud I was writing in my book! I will keep doing it. Maybe Phoebe will notice.

November 12

We went outside and I held Phoebe's hand. Her hair once went up in the wind and I got some in my mouth. I couldn't get it out and she said she didn't know why I kept spitting and making faces. She laughed!

November 13

Phoebe's daughter came in to see her. Audrey was very beautiful, just like Phoebe. She smiled at Phoebe and she even smiled at me. A nurse also came in to comb Phoebe's hair. It is so long and beautiful. I would like to comb it some-day. The doctors read my book and told me that kis has one more s.

November 14

The doctors said somebody in the next room went away on a long vacation. Somebody said it was Alice but they will not tell us exactly. They said they thought she was good enough to take her own medicine. She was smiling like normal when we went outside last time. Maybe Alice was happy to go on her vacation! I would not be happy. If I go away on vacation Phoebe will come with me.

November 15

The nurses are sad. I almost cried. Phoebe and I are both scared. I saw Alice a couple days ago when we went out-side and she talked to me and Phoebe and she didn't say anything about a long vacation. I think everyone liked Alice a lot. Everyone is acting funny. We don't want to go away like Alice. It's scary here at night. When it gets dark I hear nurses walking around and making noises but Phoebe breathes a lot in her sleep. I breathe the same time she does sometimes and that is not scary.

November 16

Phoebe always laughs at my funny jokes. I love her laugh. It takes away the scariness. I think she likes me. Maybe I'll kiss her and then she'll marry me! Here comes supper.

November 17

I KISSED HER! I KISSED HER! I KISED HER! She didn't say anything but her eyes got real wide and she giggled. My lips felt funny and a little wet. Now I feel shy but after snack I'll talk to her maybe. Hopefully I will!

November 18

Phoebe talks to me more and more after I kissed her. Maybe she likes me! I sure like her. Audrey came back but she looked sad. I think she might have been crying. I think I'll ask Phoebe why.

November 19

Today one of the doctors said he was still sad about Alice. Everybody was so sad that I cried. Phoebe made me feel better though. She told me funny stories about when Audrey was a little kid and she said Audrey always cried a lot. Once she said she was playing in the leaves a long time ago and Audrey got one in her mouth and she was cold but Phoebe helped her and she stopped crying. She promised to tell me more stories about Audrey.

November 21

I was so sick I couldn't write yesterday. The doctors said I was just tired. I was so sad because they went outside yesterday and I couldn't go. Phoebe went though. I heard her laughing outside and I wanted to kiss her outside but I was in bed. It's scary here without Phoebe.

November 22

A nurse gave me a book yesterday and I read it to Phoebe. She liked the book and laughed and laughed. I laughed too. When the bear got his head in the yellow pot of hunny she got worried and I told her it was OK, he'd be safe and he was! And she likes Eeyore pictures. She said Audrey always liked Eeyore too.

November 23

Audrey came back. Phoebe said she heard Audrey talking to the doctors a lot. We went outside again but the doctors said Phoebe wasn't good enough. I was out on the grass by the fountain wondering if Phoebe would come out. They said I had enough air and when I got back in, Phoebe was sleeping. She's still asleep now. Her hair is all over the pillow and it looks nice even when it's not combed.

November 24

Phoebe's been sleeping all day. Audrey is around a lot

lately. I told the doctor to wake Phoebe up so I could read her the book again. The doctor said no and told me to go to sleep but I'm still awake and I want Phoebe to be awake so we can talk.

November 25

The nurse put funny wires in Phoebe's nose. I tried to stop them and I said I'll wake Phoebe up, but they said no. She looks silly like that. I wonder why they don't yell "PHOEBE WAKE UP" real loud. That would work.

November 26

They closed the curtain between me and Phoebe. I can't look at her anymore and it's awful dark in here with the curtain closed so I get scared. A lot of people are in the room near Phoebe. They are all talking about her. She should wake up soon. My food is here.

November 27

Audrey was crying again. I can hear it. She cries loud. I asked the nurse why and she told me to go to sleep and not worry about it but I yelled real loud. I just wanted to wake Phoebe up. I hate the doctors when they don't tell me why they closed the curtain and why I can't read Phoebe the book again and why so many people always stay near Phoebe and I can't.

November 28

I get so mad because they never open the curtain. I just want to see Phoebe again. Maybe she would laugh at the

Eeyore pictures. I could comb her hair too and maybe she can tell me more funny stories about Audrey playing around in the cold in the leaves. But I can't even talk to her if they don't wake her up!

November 29

I still can't see through the curtain. She has not laughed lately. When I kissed her long time ago she laughed and she even laughed once when her hair was in my mouth. I want to see her. She has not laughed lately. I might be sneaky tomorrow.

November 30

Today in the morning I got out of bed very quiet and I started to touch the curtain to see Phoebe. A nurse saw me and she was very mad and she pushed me away hard and said they will do bad things to me if I try to touch Phoebe and they won't let me outside anymore and she yelled about shocks and electricity. I never even saw Phoebe! I wanted to say I was just trying to wake her up and read the Eeyore book and maybe kis her. They would not listen. They told me to go to sleep.

November 31

PIPE SMOKE

by Emily Clark, *Puyallup, Washington*

I sat on Wilbur's lap, purring softly, dreaming of my younger days, when mice were abundant and cat food was unheard of for supper. A fire crackled before us pleasantly, making the tiny cottage cozy and warm, while rain streamed down the window panes. Above me, Wilbur's newspaper rustled softly, and the smell of the ink filled my nostrils. Less pleasant was the tobacco smoke from his pipe, but I bore that uncomplainingly as I knew Wilbur loved these moments shared together as much as I did, probably more. No, I thought, I didn't long for the mouse-hunting days; this was much nicer, calm, peaceful, and you didn't have to move. For his part, Wilbur seemed to have no problem with that. I looked up at him now, the newspaper lay over his face, for he had dozed off. The pipe drooped precariously out of his mouth. I hoped he wouldn't drop it. Once before he had, and it had taken days to get the nasty-tasting tobacco out of my soft fur.

Just in case, I rose up to my feet and managed to stretch high enough to nuzzle his chin. He awoke with a start, dropping his pipe, but luckily I dodged it.

"Oh, drat," he muttered, and gathered up the spilled tobacco. He laid it, along with the pipe on the lamp table and followed me into the adjoining kitchen.

"Marjorie," he asked, "milk or sardines?" I had no idea

what his curious babble meant, but I knew by his tone that he loved me. I hoped there would be sardines for dinner tonight.

"Sorry we're out of sardines. Here's your bowl of milk. There's a little mincemeat pie left, I'll share it with you." Apparently, I did not have to suffer cat-food tonight. Most days I was lucky to get gravy over it.

Wilbur sat at the table and set a dish of the pie beside my milk. After the quiet snack, he murmured, "Good-night, Marjorie," and wheezed a couple of times. I rubbed against his legs, purring as he scratched the top of my head. I followed him to the stairs, which were set between the kitchen and the sitting room. There were no other rooms in the cottage except for Wilbur's bedroom and bathroom, both upstairs. I did not ascend the steps, which were narrow and dark. Wilbur was even older than I and likely to stumble over me, doing neither of us any good should he fall.

Instead, I padded back into the kitchen and, with a carefully judged leap, I settled myself in the window. Because of the rain, I could not see outdoors, but I wasn't really interested in that.

I thought of the time I first met Wilbur, or tried to. But I couldn't remember, although I knew there had been a short time before him. I thought of his solitary bachelorhood. I used to wish he would marry a plump, jovial woman who could bake pies and hum snatches from little tunes. Now, I had grown used to life as it was and would have resented any change. My thoughts wandered on, and gradually I dozed off. Usually, I climb up the stairs to sleep, curled up at the foot of Wilbur's bed.

I awoke suddenly and with a start. I could not be sure what it was that awakened me. It was still dark outside but no longer raining. Then my ears caught the sound of Wilbur's coughing. I hurried up the dark stairs, and stood in the doorway. Wilbur lay on the bed groaning. I heard him wheeze my name. His eyes caught sight of me and he seemed pleased at my presence, but then he rolled on his side, heaving another cough. It was the last sound he would ever make. I stood motionless in the doorway. I understood. Slowly, I turned and padded downstairs. I felt a dull ache all over, and with a last look in the direction of the steps, I knew I would never see him again.

NAMELESS
by Christy Crouch, *Temple, Texas*

When we met he called me by name;
after a while he called me friend;
more time passed he called me best friend;
a couple dates later he called me girlfriend;
as the relationship progressed he started calling
me sweetheart;
at the peak of our existence he called me love;
then we argued, he called me stubborn;
now quite a bit later he doesn't call at all.

LOVE: ASSIMILATION OF TWO WORLDS

by Cindy Duong, *Los Angeles, California*

Mai mat goc roi. Though this phrase may be spoken in Vietnamese, it equates the same idea whether in English, French, Dutch, Swahili, Spanish or Korean. You've lost your roots.

Many young adults who immigrated to America when they were small or belong to first born generations of parents who immigrated to America, face the issue of cultural conflict. Can the child brought up in the traditional values of one's native homeland also live in American society, used to American values?

For many, not only do they face racial bigotry from others, but discrimination from their own ethnic group. Taunts and jeers that they are being traitors, too Americanized, or not loyal to their homeland are some of the things they encounter.

Love, for people who find themselves caught in this situation, means accepting that you cannot let the emotional upheaval divide you. It means finding a point of mutual understanding and respect between two worlds in order to form one's singular culture.

Ever since I could remember, others have criticized me for not being the "traditional" Vietnamese girl. At school, I have friends of all ethnic groups. Yet, when most Vietnamese people realize that I am Vietnamese, they mock me

Cindy Duong

for not hanging around with "my own kind." Constantly, others would question me on why I would not speak in Vietnamese or why I insist on using an American name rather than my Vietnamese one.

What I hated about these situations was they would not listen to my rationale. First, I speak English because my friends could understand it and yet I do speak Vietnamese to some. But the main reason I do not speak the language is because most of the Vietnamese people I talk to say that I have a funny accent.

I also feel, like many who have changed their names, that I did so because it is easier to pronounce. If people could correctly pronounce my name, Trang (chahng), I would not care if they called me by that. However, listening to people call me "Throng" or "Tang" exasperated me.

However, for most people who go through such conflicts, the problems are not merely at school, they occur at home. Some may be criticized or forbidden by parents to speak English. Many parents expect the child to act the traditional child which causes conflict, because American ideas and the old country's traditional views differ. For example, in the Vietnamese culture, parents often expect to plan out their children's lives, from what their career will be to whom they will marry; yet, most people brought up in American society want the right to choose for themselves. When this conflict occurs, as it often does in my house, the individual then suffers from misunderstandings and scorn.

Can an individual live such a life? In his article *Back To*

LOVE: ASSIMILATION OF TWO WORLDS

Bachimba, Enrique Hank Lopez wrote of his experiences of growing up in America, although born in Mexico. He said "I must reconcile myself to schizo-cultural limbo, with a mere hyphen to provide some slight cohesion between my split selves. This inevitable splitting is a plague and a pleasure." So, there may be negative aspects that make *this* situation a plague because what others say can often lead to anger and resentment; but just because others question *your* ethics and values does not mean that you should reject your own. If Lopez can use the often derogatory term *pocho* which suggests that one's lost one's Mexican heritage, in a positive way to mean "up-rooted Mexican," I can use the term *mai mat goc* to mean enhancing one's culture, rather than losing one's roots. Thus, love constitutes the acceptance that you do not have to please others. Rather than play tug-of-war between two cultures, pull the two together to form a unique one of your own. No, you are not giving in to compromise, but combining the best of two worlds into your unique own.

In the end, whether you're Asian-American, African-American, Latino, or other, you can rightly say to yourself: because of me, because I have decided to make use of both the American and my native land's customs, America can continue to carry on its traditions while enhancing its and my own culture by inspiring the multi-ethnicity that has made it what it is today.

ONLY SEARCHING FOR THE PERFECT OUTFIT
by Emily Luce, *San Francisco, California*

Today
in the dressing room of The Gap
Rukiya said
"You are so in love"
and I just smiled
a little worried that you
would hear.
You didn't say anything though.
I wonder
how cold your hand really was
when you put it in the pocket
of your coat
that I was wearing —
you made me wear it
so I wouldn't be cold.
You scared me
because
what if you touched my face like that
because you wanted to
touch somebody?
The day became a series
of little tests.
You did ok
I guess.
And you blew me a kiss goodbye.

ONLY SEARCHING FOR THE PERFECT OUTFIT

You crazy boy
at least
you gave me
sweet dreams.

LOVE AT FIRST SIGHT

by Christine Ratliff, *New Lexington, Ohio*

Ever hear the old expression "love at first sight"? Does it hold any truth? Can you actually look at someone and decide that you want to spend the rest of your life with him? Is love really based on a person's nose or hair color? Superficial love, maybe, but certainly not true love.

Yeah, through high school, guys you never knew really wanted to date you. Why? Because you had a beautiful face and a dynamite figure to match. It's like matching socks, one blue goes with the other blue.

You still sleep with your blankie, the one that you can't sleep without. Do they know that? Would they still want to date you if they found out?

The point I'm trying to make is love is more than a head of bobbling blonde curls and a bra size that's bigger than the I.Q....

How much more? If a girl was dog meat and had a great personality, would you still like her? Most guys say "yes," but is that really true? Think about it.

Do you seriously think you can have a relationship with a bimbo? I know she's pretty, but does she know four plus four is eight, and not nine?

Can you be in love with that? Wouldn't you rather have someone who has a brain and knows how to use it?

Packages are pretty to look at, but can you really deeply love just the wrapping and not what's underneath?

FOR THE LOVE OF THE GAME

by Anne Miller, *Salisbury, Maryland*

It was one of those hot, muggy nights that come only in late August. The sun was setting, sending out its last glittering rays to reflect off of the river and the marsh across the way. I was sitting on the dock, my back against a pile of innertubes that my father and I had used earlier that day, and I knew that if I only turned around, I would still see my mother in the window, cleaning up the dinner dishes.

My ever present radio was by my side, tuned to the local station that carried all the games of my favorite baseball team, the Baltimore Orioles. Sitting on the quiet dock, listening to the music of the cicadas and the crickets, I could almost imagine they were the voices of the crowds at the stadium. And the luminescent sun — it was the bright illumination of the ballpark's night lights shining down upon the vibrant field....

"Candy! Get your cotton candy! Cotton candy!"

The voices of the vendors mingled with the tumult of the crowd, creating a deafening din that we could hear even as we were loosening up, playing sockball in the hallway that led to the dugout. Even without looking, we knew the stadium was filled to capacity. People of all shapes and sizes had come to watch us, their favorite team, clinch the American League pennant. We were playing the Chicago White Sox, hoping for a chance at the World Series. So far both teams had played amazingly well, and the tally stood at three games apiece.

By eleven o'clock the score was tied. It was one all in the bottom of the ninth on this horribly cold and damp Monday night in October. You couldn't tell though, at least not by the 40,000-some fans still in attendance. The most amazing part was their enthusiasm. Even on a night like this, and even though I was seated on the dugout bench, I felt like I could just reach out and grab hold of the energy emitted from the stands.

"Hey Chris!"

It was the manager calling me over.

"Get ready, son. I'm sending you in to hit for Stevey. Go to it!"

No sooner had he uttered those words than my heart rate skyrocketed. I hadn't played for over a month, much less sat on the bench, courtesy of a bad knee. And now the skipper was sending me out to pinch hit?

"Go on out there already, boy! We're countin' on ya!" I chose my favorite bat from the rack in the corner. Nodding to the batboy, I sauntered calmly onto the field. As soon as my foot touched the grass, a silent hush fell upon the spectators. Could they feel my pulse racing too? Could they see the rapid rise and fall of my panting chest? Did they too possess that small, lingering doubt, that after so long, I might not be able to perform like I used to?

Marching up to the batter's box, I took a few practise swings as I went. Eventually I reached the plate. Slowly, carefully, I put one foot into the batter's box and dug my cleats in. The other foot came next, spaced carefully to the side. Resting the bat against my shoulder, I assumed my traditional stance. I tried vainly to block out the whispers of the crowd, the stadium's glaring lights, the subtle shifting of the Sox defense. Concentrate on that one mean figure on the mound, I told myself. I tried to unnerve him as I glared through the mean slits of my eyes, waiting for the pitch — a fastball that caught me looking.

"STEE-RIKE ONE!" yelled the umpire. I turned and glowered at him too for a moment before stepping away from the plate. Wasting time, I leaned back and focused on the bat I held upright before my eyes. Concentrate! I told myself again. Stepping back next to the plate, ready to once again try and unnerve the pitcher, I became acutely aware of how deafening the silent crowd had become.

This time, as I tried to stare down the pitcher yet again, something changed. The lights grew dimmer. The crowd and the fielders became eerily silent and still, almost nonexistent. And as the figure on the mound smirked back at me and started his delivery, I knew I had him. He threw the last pitch, a fastball. *Big mistake.* I saw it rise, ever so slowly, into the air after I hit it, turning and spinning on its way over the fence. Suddenly, in a rush, it all came back. The fans were going wild, screaming and yelling so loud I swore they could hear it in Washington. The lights came back on full strength, illuminating the shocked faces of the Sox players. I jogged easily around the diamond with the world's biggest grin on my face. I had done it — we had done it! Watch out Reds!

Anne Miller

Cincinatti, here we come!
 ..."Chris, Chris! Are you listening to another baseball game?"
 "Yeah, Mom."
 "Why don't you turn off that radio for once and come in? It's just a game, for Heaven's sake!"
 Just a game? Ah, mothers. What do they know?

HOURGLASS LOVE

by Annesa Lee, *Honolulu, HI*

When we started out, the hourglass was full
But slowly as the sands grew less and less
    so did your love.
I ask you one thing as the last few grains
    of sand disappear...
Just as the hourglass is turned over...
When it is empty — could we start over?

PEBBLES IN THE OCEAN

by Megan Edwards, *New Bern, North Carolina*

I am like a pebble being shaped by
the waves of life in the ocean of
the world.

The wave is my friend. It smooths
my rough edges. It massages my
harshness away.

This wave makes me beautiful; shiny,
pink and delicate. It gives me a
splendor that is seen by all.

With true fondness and admiration
I cling to the wave. It shelters
me from all the dangers of the
ocean.

Yet once the wave has gained my faith, it tosses me
        against the
jagged rocks on the beach and
bruises my once immaculate spirit.

I lie there, harsh, and again with
many rough and sharp edges.

I lie among shards of other broken
pebbles, waiting.

Soon another wave comes and embraces me in its pure
    white foam.

It gently picks me up off the beach
and slowly begins to smooth my
coarse edges.

The new wave washes my bitterness
away. It cleanses my stained spirit.

I eventually begin to give this new wave
my trust.

Hoping, praying, knowing, that this
time it will be different.

This time I will not be shattered.

A MOTHER'S TRIUMPH
by Jenika Jessen, *Paris, Idaho*

"Sheblik!" The scream echoed through the night, but was met by the heavy silence of the savannah. Desperate fear surged through Kantara's body as she frantically searched the plains for her lost foal. The sound of Kantara's heavy breathing and pounding hoof beats disturbed the silence of the open expanses. The wind rushed in her ears as onward she ran, determined not to rest until her foal was found.

She stopped, straining her ears for an answer to her desperate cry. Hearing nothing, she prepared herself to run out, but stopped. There, in the distance, was the faint but unmistakable cry of a hyena. She turned to face the sound and stood silently, hoping to catch the sound again. The screaming was closer this time, and the meaning of it sent a chill through her body. She bolted furiously toward the cry and prayed that she was not too late.

Sheblik stared helplessly at the face of the hyena. Many times he had seen the torn bodies of young such as himself that had fallen prey to the ruthless jaws of a ravenous pack of hyenas or the claws of a lioness, but never had he thought that their fate might someday be his own until now.

Shezar swung his head around and was met by the eager face of his pack. Venemously he laughed, then spoke triumphantly, "Here we have the foal of Kantara. Your mother is a bitter enemy of mine son, and we have hated one another for a very long time. It looks like the score will finally be evened.''

He even laughed victoriously, the pack laughing with him.

''You won't get away with this Shezar. Zari will protect me.''

Shezar laughed uproariously then spat at the young Zebra scornfully, ''Bah, you think your weak God will save you? When my pack is through with you there won't be anything left but a dirty pile of bones.''

The pack gathered in closer, anxious to begin their much-awaited feast. Sheblik shuddered in horror as the ravenous jaws of Shezar descended on him.

Furiously, Kantara rushed toward the voices. Her mind was racing, something was wrong, very desperately out of place, and then it struck her — that voice, she knew that voice. It was the voice that had haunted her dreams as a foal, it was the voice that had countless times woken her from her sleep, screaming. That voice belonged to the dog that had killed her mother. Rage surged through her like hot lead. Blinded by her anger, she crashed through the brush and into the thicket that concealed the pack of hyenas.

With screams of panic the hyenas scrambled away from the creature that had come smashing through the thicket. Never letting his paw leave the neck of the struggling baby zebra beneath him, Shezar whirled to face the intruder. Then he saw her. ''So it is you, Kantara.'' He spoke her name with contempt. As you know, we have some business that was never settled and I was just about to take it up with your foal."

The scattered members of the pack slowly edged closer to Kantara, forming a deadly circle around the mare and their leader. "Let him go, Shezar, this is between you and me. What was started many moons ago will be ended tonight." Kantara spoke with cold determination.

With a growl of anger Shezar shoved Sheblik from him. Gasping for air, the foal struggled unsteadily to his feet. Shezar growled "I should have killed you when I killed your mother."

Kantara chuckled without humor "You should have known that a foal can be vicious when fighting for its life. It's too bad that instead of killing you, I only took your eye."

The fact that he had lost his eye to a zebra had constantly eaten at his soul until it had become an obsession. He had vowed never to rest until he had gotten revenge, and now his time had come "Kill her!"

The screams of the attacking hyenas filled the night. Their short, razor-sharp teeth ripped through the hide of their quarry. Struggling to keep her balance, Kantara fought as only a mother can when she is protecting her young. But ten to one is impossible odds, even for one fighting with her fury, and soon she could feel herself giving in to the terrible jaws of the pack.

Kantara felt her hind legs buckle and desperately struggled to keep her footing, in a last pleading prayer she cried "Please, Zari, spare me!"

A hyena fell to the ground screaming with pain and, as if the pain were contagious, the others followed, howling. Painfully, Kantara climbed to her feet. "Get up you fools! Kill her! She is one and you are many. Get up before I..." His eyes glazed and foam began to froth at his cheeks. His chest constricted in a vain attempt to draw air, then he fell... dead.

The hounds of the pack whimpered in fear as they stared at the dead body of their leader, and then, howling their loss, they ran into the night.

A small light flickered in front of the two lone zebras. Steadily the light continued to grow brighter. Nickering nervously, the pair shied away from the light. Slowly, the light began to gather in one spot and the form of a zebra flickered in the air in front of Kantara and Sheblik. With increasing anxiety, Kantara nudged Sheblik away from the light.

The light that emanated from the figure now glowed with such intensity that neither of the zebras could bear to look directly at it. The voice echoed in her mind "Kantara, daughter of Mandoz and Reshab, you have fought well. Stand forth and receive thy reward, Little Sister." Slowly, with great reverence, she approached the figure, head bowed with respect. "This shall be yours, and all yours, for generations to come, a sign to mark the victory of the zebra over its foe, the hyena. Stripes of black night and purest white I give you. Wear them proudly. To the hyena I give brown spots of cowardice and deceit, that all might know the nature of this creature."

Kantara looked down and gasped. Gone were the bloody wounds that had been inflicted by the hyenas, and in their place stood the majestic stripes which she had been promised. Humbly, she fell to her knees in an expression of awed gratitude.

"Peace be with you, Little Sister." The words of the zebra echoed in her mind. Together, silently, they watched the light slowly dissipate, and then it was gone.

OLD BALDY
by David R. Patterson, *Statesville, North Carolina*

Old Baldy stared down at me in the distance. Huge and distinctively groomed, he waited for us to approach him. His head was unabashedly barren. Creative combing, plugs, toupees, and The Hair Club for Men were for lesser, more insecure beings who foolishly feared the loss of youth and physical beauty with each fallen follicle. Baldy did not consider Father Time to be his mortal enemy, in fact, he might have been the Father's wild brother. He had shaved with glaciers and had told the pioneers to take another route; he was not frightened that a vain, manipulative creature would emblazon TRUMP on him any more than you or I would be frightened that a lone worker ant would build The Sears Towers of ant hills on our foreheads. Old Baldy was undaunted by time and history.

But I am not. I had the privilege of meeting this monument to nature's majesty last summer in northern New Mexico. Hungry for travel and eager to see the untouched wonders of the West, I signed up for a twelve day camping trip at the Philmont Scout Ranch, located in the Sangre de Cristo Mountains. My friends and I hiked the ninety miles of rough terrain with our homes, grocery stores, and hospitals on our backs. We all knew that Old Baldy, the nearly 13,000 foot peak, would be the climax of the trip. We set out in a rush to reach it, to savor every moment and view.

David R. Patterson

The hike through Baldly's beard of trees seemed endless. As soon as we hit the rock cap everyone dispersed and breathed it in for themselves. Old Baldy wasn't so bald after all. Moss, lichen, and wildflowers were anchored to the cracks in the rocks and swung rhythmically in the wind. I even saw a ten-point buck lazily wandering a hundred yards in front of me.

The eye-straining view, the top-of-the-world height, and rugged, delicate beauty were more than I had anticipated. My exhilaration, though, was bittersweet as I realized that I could see radio towers and an airport down below. Although Old Baldy stubbornly refuses to be domesticated, the land beneath and beyond it is losing its natural face to man's tattoos and cosmetic surgeries. It goes beyond just the inevitable change; this is destruction. From the top of this old fortress I could see man advancing. He is fighting an undeclared war, an unintentional war with the Planet Earth. He is winning every battle and losing more and more with each victory. Old Baldy may be fearless, but I am not.

FIFTIES LOVE STORY

by Carey King, *New Bern, North Carolina*

Shoo - bop - de - wop - de - wop - a - do

Sweet sixteen, she fell in love
blond hair, blue eyes
on the wrong side of the tracks
motorcycle jacket.

She - wop - a - do.

Class ring, school jacket
going steady
staying out late
gossip, gossip, gossip.

De - wop - a - do.

Drive-in movies
Ford Fairlane
stalling on the tracks
train coming, they die
sweet love.

Shoo - bop - a - de - wop - a - dooooo.

DIAMOND MEMORIES
by Ryan Montgomery, *Houston, Texas*

"You have to be a man to be a big leaguer, but you have to a have a lot of little boy in you, too."

—Roy Campanella

I can't quite recall the sound of the ball off the bat that spring morning, but I do remember my legs kicking into gear beneath me as I moved to field it and all the excitement of an eight year-old-ball player churning inside of me. This was one of those opportunities that I craved all season long.

It wasn't much of a hit — the kind that died when it got into the air, not headed any place but down. Playing first base, I had already snagged one ball that inning, and I couldn't believe my good fortune at getting another chance for stardom so soon. I sprinted toward my prey with all the speed I could muster, as sure of myself as a kid can be.

I can still feel my glove slipping a couple of inches off my hand when I hit the ground. But it stayed on. And the ball was safely inside.

"Good catch," admitted the opposing team's coach, as the parents burst into cheers.

For some reason, that's the only full inning that sticks in my mind from seven seasons of baseball.

A few weeks ago, I visited the field on which I caught that ball years ago. I could tell that baseball season hadn't begun, for the grass growing up in the base paths looked unkept, and only patches of dirt remained on the four corners and the mound. It certainly didn't appear worthy of an organized sport. Then again, it never really did, even when I played on it every week during springtime. The grass has always been some kind of odd mixed breed, unique to this place; cracks cut through the ground in various areas, wreaking havoc on the infielders; the backstop behind home plate served as a dugout for both teams; and our parents brought lawn chairs to form makeshift rows a few feet off the first and third baselines. In fact, the only parts that gave our game any shreds of legitemacy were the umpires, chalk base lines and real bases.

This was the best that the Alief YMCA had to offer. We didn't know any better. All we wanted was a place to play.

At least that's all I wanted.

Now the only kind of baseball I know is the kind on television. The last time I picked up a bat seems like ages ago. And my old glove just hangs on the wall, looking pretty beaten-up, weary, and nostalgic.

Maybe I'll never rekindle the joy I had on a baseball field. I certainly won't find it on T.V. But that's okay. As a kid the sport was everything; as you get older, there are other paths to happiness. Now it's my younger brother's turn to make the plays, get the cheers, and hear the coach say ''Good catch.''

Whatever happens, I'll never forget the backstop fields. I'll never forget the time when tossing a baseball back and forth with my dad was about the greatest fun I could imagine. I'll never forget the game.

JOHN MARTIN
by Scott Francar, *Green Bay, Wisconsin*

One day not so long ago, a man named John Martin was walking down a street in the city. He hated everyone and everything. He was very selfish and greedy. If he saw a little kitty cat, he would kick it in the head. If he saw a bird with one wing missing, he'd tear off the other wing. What this man mostly does during the day is watch his crippled pets suffer. He has two dogs, a cat, and some mice. He feeds them all once a week. Many of them have broken bones and are only half alive. He loves to just sit and watch them in their agony. Now all of this is just what he does to animals. He also loves to steal from people and cheat them.

Anyway, on the same street a man named Bob Smith was also walking toward John. When he passed John he got hit in the head with a bat and was knocked unconscious. John stole his wallet and was dragging him by the neck to a graveyard where he would bury Bob alive. Just then a police car went down the street and the policeman saw this. The policeman got out of the car and pointed his gun at John as he yelled, "You are under arrest. Drop the man and come here with your hands up."

John wasn't about to go with the cop, so he started to run while dragging Bob with him, thinking he would lose the cop. He thought wrong. The cop aimed his gun right at John's head and started to put his finger on the trigger. Then he stopped. Bob began gaining consciousness and stood up. He was right in front of John who had let him go a few seconds earlier when he had begun to groan. Bob was in between the cop and John. So the cop put the gun down. Bob was facing the cop, so upon seeing him and not John, he thought it was the cop who had knocked him out. Just as John was about to hit Bob again, Bob ran toward the cop and tackled him before he could shoot at John. John was astonished. He ran toward Bob and said, "I mugged you, stole your wallet, and was about to kill you, and you saved my life! Why?"

"Because I believe that deep down inside, you have some love for everyone, and I am trying to help you find it." Bob lied in hopes of getting his wallet back.

"Yes, yes, I found the love!" John shouted. "Here, here, take your wallet! I have to start spreading my love right now!"

He did too. First he went home and fixed up all of his pets and fed them. He gave money to the poor and the people he had cheated. He was being nice to everyone. John Martin now loves everyone and everything.

AND HE WAKES HER UP
by Ba Nguyen, *Houston, Texas*

And he wakes her up,
    saying a quiet prayer of thanks that she *does* wake
    up.
He opens the silver box that contains all her pills and
    potions:
    two red, a green, half a yellow, eyedrops, the stuff
    in the brown bottle.
None of it seems to help, but he diligently
    administers it to her,
    obediently, careful not to forget anything.

She struggles with him some mornings, but today
    she is quiet and easy.
After the morning ritual is complete, she eats
    the breakfast he made for her,
    their roles now reversed.
How are you, he asks her, just to make conversation.
    I'd be fine if I knew where I was or who
    you were, she says, her tone becoming indignant
    and hostile;

Ba Nguyen

You're home, Mom. I'm your son, Kenneth.
    His voice cracks a little, like it did the first time.
What's your name, Mom, he asks her, hoping that she'll
    remember. What's your name...
    But she only fidgets and plays with her food and
    looks away.
Your name is Mary, Mom. Your name is Mary
    Thelander.
    Your address is 3301 Amherst. You live with your
    son,
    Kenneth—I'm Kenneth. Today is Monday, August
    12th, 1989.

    Oh.

He stands there and looks at her, this shell of a
    human being that once raised and took care of him.
And as he brushes her silver and grey hair, he looks into
    her eyes, only to find nothing. No sign of
    remembrance, no sign at all.
Who are you? Where's Bill? she asks, her worry obvious.
    Dad died twenty years ago, Mom.
    Today is Monday, August 12th, 1989.

HANDS OF DARKNESS
by Bethany P. Crandell, *Springfield, Virginia*

I stared silently at the wall of my bedroom. I sat on the edge of my bed, my knees pulled up to my chin. Shivering a little, I pulled my hair into a tight knot behind my head and held it there. My eyes stung from their forced stare. I was afraid to move, afraid of what I may see if I closed my eyes for even a second. The clock across the room said that I had been this way four and a half hours. Slowly, I released my hair and lowered my head towards my knees.

Earlier in the afternoon the school bus had been on its way home from the championship basketball game, carrying the number one ranked Keating Mustangs. The team was in an absolute frenzy caused by their one point victory over the Easton Bulldogs.

"Everybody up! Sing the Alma Mater!! Show some pride!!!!" I heard the team captain shout as we rounded the corner into the school. I was surrounded by a bus load of happily sweating basketball players. We all held hands high above our heads and swayed to the song we called our own. A few of the younger players just hummed loudly while others shouted the words with such force my ears ached. Their faces were flushed, eyes bright, and mouths were agape with song. The aroma of deodorant-covered sweat permeated the bus. I sighed regretfully as we pounded the ceiling, signifying the end of our trip and our Alma Mater. A winning season was now over. I gathered my coat, scorebook, and purse then clambered off the bus with the rest of the team.

"So how's my favorite scorekeeper?" one of the players asked as he put his damp arm around me fondly. I was beginning to wish that they had showered before the bus ride. "Are you going to the victory party?" he asked as we walked into the locker room together. As the team statistician, it was customary for me to follow the team everywhere, including the locker room.

"Beth alert! Beth alert!" I heard another yell as I walked in, signifying to all that they had better keep their pants on for a few more minutes. I smiled to myself as the smallest player fell over himself trying to pull his pants up from his knees.

"Don't worry guys, I'm sure there's not much to hide anyway!" I teased. I had known almost all of them since third grade so my teasing was natural. They were like brothers to me. They threw sweat socks in my face on a regular basis, so there was no possible way that I could be considered a girl anymore. I was simply their little sister. I walked into the coach's office and closed the door behind me. The smell of gym socks and Ben Gay was not as potent in this room. I climbed over the medical kit, balls, and piles of dirty jerseys to the desk. Flopping down on the overstuffed chair, I cleared off a place for my scorebook to call in the statistics of the game. I reached out for the phone, dialing the numbers quickly.

As I sat on my bed, my hair pulled back once again, the vision of those numbers swam in my head. The blank, white wall glared back at me. "I can't think about this!" I screamed to myself. The clock kept on. I silently watched the hands turn ever so slowly. My back ached from sitting this way so long and I felt sick to my stomach. The wall in front of me played its part as the theater of my mind. The movie continued on.

I stepped out into the empty locker room. Streamers hung quietly from the ceiling and confetti covered the cold linoleum floor.

"Hello? Anyone in here?" I asked as I walked cautiously over towards the door. No one answered.

"Oh well," I said aloud as I flicked off the light in the locker room." Guess they are waiting for me outside." The door slammed hard behind me and echoed as I walked out into the deserted gym.

"Great guys! Thanks for waiting!" I thought sarcastically. "Sure hope my ride gets here soon." I was beginning to get worried. I didn't like being anywhere alone, much less an empty gymnasium. I walked hesitantly closer and closer to the door. Stopping at the heavy metal frame, I turned instinctively and retraced my steps back into the gym. It would be better to wait inside in the light rather than out in the blackness of the night.

I had a funny feeling in my stomach as I sat down on

Bethany P. Crandell

the wooden bleachers. It was as if someone else was in that gym. Shuddering slightly, I looked back over my shoulder. A bright poster-covered wall glared back defiantly. The same posters my friends and I had made earlier in the week. "Look MA... No Hands" my favorite one read. Paint covered hands of my friends and myself had lovingly covered the entire sheet of cool white paper.

I felt foolish for being so afraid. I looked around at the walls of the gym. I had never realized how big this place really was. The roar of the crowds, the sound of music at the dances, and the screams of spirit at the pep rallies all seemed to fill this place to capacity. In their absence, I felt small, insignificant.

Nervously, I glanced down at my watch. Fidgeting with my blue letter sweater, I walked over to the silver water fountain in the darkest corner of the gym. I thought I saw something move to the left of me as I bent down to drink the cool water.

Suddenly, two heavy, muscular arms reached out of the darkness and clamped my arms to my sides. One arm was wrapped around my face so that my nose, my mouth, and part of my eyes were covered, and the other arm was secured around my chest to keep my arms from breaking free. I struggled to wrench free from his grasp, but it was no use. He pulled me into his darkness and pushed me up against the cold brick wall. He let go of me only briefly, and I screamed. My cries echoed through the empty gym and out into the deserted lot beyond.

Silently, he twisted a bandana away from his neck and stuffed it forcefully into my mouth. I continued trying to scream but nothing more than a whimper came out. I could taste the dirty, stale sweat from the bandana on my lips as I closed my eyes. Warm tears squeezed out from beneath my eyelids. My stomach throbbed with fear and my head pulsed. He had grabbed both of my wrists and pinned them to the wall above my head. He held them tightly, so that the more I struggled the more pain I felt, but I continued to fight. A warm trickle of blood oozed down my arm from my wrist. With one hand he began stroking my hair, while the other still held my bruised wrists tightly. He passed his dirty finger down along my ear towards my cheek. He drew circles across my eyes and down my nose.

I could feel my body and my mind beginning to go numb. I tuned out everything. Feeling nothing, I heard the tear of my blouse. I squeezed my eyes closed tighter as the tips of his fingers traced over the tops of my breasts. My mind was blank now. I felt as if my body was weightless. Part of me drifted above myself, looking down upon the scene unfolding. I saw that revolting creature's dirt stained hands pawing my body. I saw a look of utter terror across my face, and yet, I still felt nothing. I looked up and saw nothing. The walls of the gym had disappeared. All that my eyes focused on was a blue light at the far corner of my black void. I drifted closer and closer to that light with every breath. Just as I felt the cozy warmth of it around me, I heard the blare of a horn. With that, the walls of the gym reappeared, and

Bethany P. Crandell

I came crashing back down to earth. The man must have heard it too because my arms were unpinned from the wall, and I collapsed to the ground. I heard the man's footsteps grow farther away as he ran deep into the night.

I could still hear those footsteps running through my head as I sat on the edge of my bed five and a half hours later. I could not get rid of them. They had been there through my silent car ride home, my frantic shower, and my long midnight vigil. I felt no pain, only disbelief.

It seemed as if I were a different person now. I looked around my room at the things that had been so personal to me only hours earlier that now seemed like strangers. I unfolded my legs toward the brightly carpeted floor and attempted to stand. Stars flew in front of my eyes and I grasped the heavy wooden bedpost to maintain my balance. Methodically, I walked over to my dresser.

The many trinkets I had collected over the years were carelessly arranged across the smooth surface. My eyes wandered aimlessly over them until they landed upon a paper cup meticulously torn into a spiral. The orange writing had faded over the season so that it read, ''O MUTANS!'' instead of the original'' GO MUSTANGS!'' It hung listlessly from one of the many cheerleading trophies that lined the dresser, just as it had from Jacs's hands so many months before; I snatched it up quickly and tore it into tiny little pieces. The styrofoam drifted like confetti from my furious hands onto the floor.

Catching a glimpse of one of the many photographs

taken at the recent pep rally, my anger shifted and that too was destroyed. Bits of colored photopaper now lined the floor. Homecoming. The most exciting time of the year. My gaze was fixed on the champagne flute that had been given to me as a gift from the class. Flinging my wild hand across it, it crashed to the floor, shattering into splintery pieces and intermingling with the paper and styrofoam.

Suddenly I began to cry. Streams of tears ran down my face. Blurry eyed I caught a glimpse of myself in the mirror directly in front of me. My hair was knotted and tangled. My face was void of color except for the red nose and blood-shot eyes. "I am a mess!" I thought to myself miserably. "What have I done?" I looked down at the floor in stark realization. Some of my most favorite possessions were now destroyed.

I knelt carefully to the ground and picked up the larger pieces of the champagne glass. Placing them gingerly on the dresser, I inventoried the pieces, but felt the frustration rise within me as the pieces simply would not fit together, too many key elements were missing. Exhausted I collapsed back onto the floor. Images raced through my mind. It seemed that I too was missing the key elements to put myself back together.

Suddenly my hand grazed something sharp. I looked over and there, under the frame of the dresser, was a large piece of glass. Picking it up I rose and attempted to place it in the puzzle of glass I had made. A glimmer of hope rose within me. With a lot of glue, patience, and determination,

I knew I could put most of this beautiful champagne flute back together. It wouldn't be the same as it was before I broke it, for some pieces were gone forever, and yet, I knew it would be strong enough to once again stand tall among the trophies and trinkets my room displayed. And though that stranger had taken parts of me when he ran away into the night, he had left enough to rebuild.

I glanced once again over at the clock. The hands told me softly that it was time for rest. I climbed under the cool sheets. They felt different somehow. Maybe they weren't as soft as they had been before, or maybe it was all in my perception. My sense of perception had changed a lot in the last few hours. I was more aware, more sensitive to things around me. That man, although he had never spoken a word, had changed my view of myself and of the world, forever.

ENCOUNTERS I-VI
by Sarah Althea Braun, *Beacon, New York*

I. diner

She saw him in the booth and sat down next to me without saying hello and I looked at her face, burned feature by feature into my brain. Short cropped hair, dark and damp, twisted into absent shapes by artist fingers to frame her thin pale face, her pale fear. Her eyes like frozen tornado sky betray her defiant vulnerability. Here I am, hurt me, she says. I've learned to take it. She cannot capture our world with the camera on her chest — two AM diner life fades to dreary countertop tan before she can adjust her focus, snap the shutter. Her words are honest, bitter, nearly cruel. Her insomnia slackened voice for some reason mentions me and that she has met a woman, she wants to have an affair, and I would too, and since she is boring us, she will be going, but I only hear the intensity, the vibrant suppression of the words that echo over the jukebox absently crooning about this "brown eyed girl". She is and has the only focus unknowingly commanding my every emotion with her insistent beauty.

II. party

She comes in somehow without smiling look at her realize her presence weight resting on those gathered tired of the dance appropriate infatuation falters under pressure by resentment domination stroll in stroll by judge sit down get up say a few words I misunderstand attempt a look at her pale face my pale fear creates accusations conscious of my clothes hair face I hide beneath my flowered hat in her smart slacks belt and shirt brilliant kerchief correctly flowing from her alabaster brow she does not sneer at the costume I made and wear for my own sake.

III. store

We come for Eden's foods; your swords flame in the window. You wait while we cross no man's land, heart pounding. The chilled air hits me and already I do not want this. I attempt denial of the bite I have taken resting in my mouth and become fascinated by rows of cookbooks, cashew butter, almonds waiting to be milked. Your form shakes, speaks, distracting.

Confrontation logic leaves only images remembered — forward art-strung lusty men filing by with their tahini. "This other guy" you call them all as they gaze into your eyes.

Premonition tells me that this stop will detain, deny us the beauty of the pot shop and the earth mother tonight. Analyzing your anatomical Darwinistic paranoias, trying to impressively ease your pain without taking sides I realize in a glance at my lovers yes that I've kissed you by the transitive property.

I run from your grating voices into stacks of ancient Chinese teas — a cure for every ill — I read the labels.

A couple, we play for a disguise. I dodge his cart and sit on it. Secure in our alliance we pay, joke, leave, lying on good terms.

IV. phone

She called my house, coitus interruptus. She knew I would suspend all my plans to understudy a canoe ride and this other guy.

V. park

I didn't expect her to be so beautiful again. I've forgotten now the color of her shirt, and her car, and the shape of her silver pendant but she was stunning against the grass and she was a woman among my friends. I try to flaunt my own greater curves to remind them, but she gets her map drawn by his hands which should be nearer me, fulfills her obligations and glides away. We all have watched her go.

VI. leaving

I damned the flood and shook out my hair when I saw her car in his driveway. I know my knees were shaking as addresses were exchanged over suitcases filled with his clothes, and some of ours. The wake of a tearing embrace between two people changed kept me from going into the room where you were and trying to talk again. Outside Nathaniel's door for the last time for a long time with "drive safely" ringing in our ears you let yourself sob and we mourned together for slipping opportunity and lost love.

MY FIRST LOVE
by Sarah Boucher, *Port Huron, Michigan*

From my snow covered window I watch
the hustle of the North
the parting of lips into a forced smile
trying to look friendly
but not having enough time to try hard
it's too cold
to stop and talk

From my snow covered window I remember
my first love
it had real smiles
and always an accompanying wave
strangers asking about your well being
and seeming to care

Everyone moving with a slow, comfortable step
and speaking with a similar drawl
it's always warm, even through rare flurries of snow
The South

The North is for some
those who love glistening fields of freshly fallen snow
and crystals of ice forming miles of prisms
surrounded by frozen ripples of water,
but the South is for me
with its mountains of green
on fire in the fall
and its forever shining sun
filling me with enough warmth to share.
Sundays at a friend's farm
where leaves always burn
and grits always cook
the fireplace is the gathering spot.

I've been pulled away
but I'll always return

Passion runs deep in my veins
for my first home
and my first love

The South.

BASEBALL
by Bethany P. Crandell, *Springfield, Virginia*

The crack of the bat,
the slice of the ball,
the pack of the glove,
it's winner takes all.

The salt on your lips,
the sun in your eyes,
the dust in your throat,
the losers heave sighs.

The victory, the loss
the thrill of it all,
can only be found
In the game of Baseball.

REINCARNATION

by Kristen Kochel, *Sumner, Washington*

Perhaps reincarnation is not a myth, but merely a time from where we get our instincts. I remember a place far different from where I've grown up, rolling plains and long wavy grasses blowing in hot summer breezes. Winters with snow driving fiercely into my face and the hushed silence after a blizzard. I see these places when I dream, images my subconscious remembers and recreates to tempt me into fully believing I am there again.

I dream of a man, as most hormone-driven teenagers do, but the things I feel are not wholly lust. I never seem to be able to see his face clearly, but I know his eyes are a deep, chocolate brown that I drown in every time I am captured by his gaze. His hair is the satiny black color of a raven's wing; it shimmers in the light, daring me to tangle my fingers in its beautiful length. It reaches his shoulder blades and will soon rival the length of my own. He has strong, capable hands with a beautiful texture put there by years of work and play. Their strength is hidden beneath a gentleness like silk-swathed steel, a steel that protects and cares for those less capable.

He has a rigid sense of honor which irritates me to no end at times; I remain virtuous by his incredible control. I could perhaps convince him otherwise in today's world, but alas, this is a dream. Once I am committed, I will not be able to back off. What he takes, when it's freely given, he keeps forever.

I believe he was a plainsman, Lakota or Cheyenne, before the Civil War. He was a warrior and was considered a member of high society, giving freely to those who didn't have enough, as is the way among the tribes. I believe he was my husband and that I was one of the tribe, whether an adopted member or born of the people.

I do not know his name; I search for it each time I dream of him. The only thing I find is the vision of a hawk, flying on a sky of red, screaming defiance at the wind and at those who cannot fly. I come back from the vision and fall prey to his heart-stopping smile.

If true love exists, could this be it? I haven't met the actual person; perhaps I never will. Is he out there dreaming of me? I can only hope he is. So many questions floating through my head and no answers to be found. My heart aches for someone, perhaps the someone of my dreams.

IN LOVING MEMORY
by Brian Tucker, *Houston, Texas*

When I first began high school I was very unsure of many things, but I knew, for certain, I would never turn my back on my friends. Just like my mother, who was a missionary at our church, I felt that God created all men equally and that for that reason all men, whether rich or poor, should be helped when they are suffering, either by charity or volunteer work.

It was amazing how for many years the ideology my mother brought me up under was not tested until I reached high school and met my future best friend, Oliver. He was a great friend — he was always there for me when I was in trouble at school, tutoring me in the subjects I was failing, and he also listened to my family troubles when I needed his help. But it was not until two years later that I had to prove my loyalty to him. This was the year that my dear friend Oliver contracted the AIDS virus.

When I found out that Oliver had AIDS, I'll admit at first, I did not really know how to treat him, but I soon learned later that you treat someone that has AIDS just like you would treat any other person — like a person; for, it is not the person we are trying to get rid of; it is the disease. At this point in my life, reality struck and I had to realize life is full of many pleasure but with it comes many pains. I also began finding out all the information I could on the disease to start educating myself about it. My Mom told me this would help me when I came across people that had no knowledge about the disease, just fear, and that maybe I would be able to educate them too.

Little did I know just how ignorant people could be. My friends did not seem open minded about learning about the disease — they had already made their decision, the one their parents instilled in them. Oliver, on the other hand, continued to go to school, but it became harder and harder for him to want to stay there because all of his friends had basically deserted him except for me. This was mainly because their parents felt that if they were around Oliver, they would contract the disease too. From that moment, I decided that I would ask the principal to set up a seminar on AIDS education for the parents — knowing that this probably would do nothing for Oliver's cause, but I was not about to give up without a fight. This idea was put into action an hour before school started the next day, but needless to say not many parents showed up because they had already gotten together the night before and decided that Oliver should be put on a home bound program.

That night Oliver found out that the parents of his friends wanted him to leave school and he called me and asked me to come over to talk to him. When I got to Oliver's house he was very ill and he seemed very lonely. I asked him what was on his mind. He asked me to sit down because he wanted to tell me how I was a very good friend even though all his other friends deserted him. He also recited a poem to me on how he felt about the world. Not until he read this poem did I realize that he was at the point of giving up his fight, and that he really wished that he was already dead, so the suffering would be over.

The poem Oliver read to me that night was entitled "Solitude" by Ella Wheeler Wilcox.

> Laugh, and the world laughs with you;
>
> Weep, and you weep alone

It seemed to me at one point of my life, that I was actually helping fight Oliver's battle. But I realized I would never know how much pain and fighting you have to go through when you are the one that is forced to face the fight. That night I watched Oliver pass before my eyes, but in my heart I knew it was for the best. At least this way, he would be free from his agony on earth. And even though he is gone, his memory will live on for all those people who loved him. I just wish I could have told him that he meant the world to me, and that when he passed away a part of me would go with him.

Afterword

In this essay, I wanted people to understand that these people are dying and need our help, but most of all they need the help of their family, friends, and loved ones. I want people to understand how much these people want help, but can not seem to get any help mainly because of fear. Many people seem to forget that there is a large percentage of society that is affected by this disease, but what we as a society need to remember is that these numbers represent real people — all of them, all of you, and all of us.

THE LONER
by Zach Roberts, *Chandler, Oklahoma*

I've been called a loner,
one to never be held down,
now I want to keep on riding,
but I need to settle down.

I'm just a simple cowboy,
like I've been for life,
here hidden by a west wind veil
from the world's pain and strife.

I'm not the one to be held down,
I live no strings attached,
I'd always thought I'd been around
then my world came unpatched.

She seemed to walk right in my life
with no shadow and no sign,
she wanted me to take it slow
and leave my ranching behind.

She doesn't seem to understand
that ranching keeps me strong,
that I need to be on open land,
and free to ride along.

Now I'm torn from inside out,
my love is ripped apart,
I know how bad I need the range,
but I also need her heart.

Now I'm caught right in between
my woman or my life,
I need to choose to let her go
or take her as my wife.

That choice sure isn't easy
if your life's as large as mine;
I can't say for sure who I need to please,
I hope I know in time.

MY FRIEND "LOVE"

by Emily Gilreath, *Apex, North Carolina*

"Grandpa," I say, "it's raining outside. The park is all wet and my toys aren't so much fun any more." Grandpa picks me up and takes me out to the garage and sets me down on the laundry basket. Then he says "Now, then, Lizzie, you shut your pretty little eyes real tight. No peeking, now because I have a surprise for you." So I close my eyes real tight and sit in the dark. I smell Nana's old hat boxes, pipe tobacco, old tires, laundry soap and fabric cleaner. I smell the memories that are stuffed in Nana's shoe boxes and cedar chests. The memories are strong and sweet and they tickle my nose.

Grandpa then says, "All right Lizzie, you can open your eyes now!" The surprise is my friend, Love! He is not like my friends in Mrs. Barker's class at preschool. Love is as tall as Grandpa, and he wears clothes just like Grandpa, but Love surely doesn't look like Grandpa! His face is all white, just like my ghost costume from Halloween, and Love has big blue stars around his eyes and a red squeaky nose.

I suddenly realize that Grandpa isn't in the garage, so I ask Love if he knows where Grandpa went. Love shrugs his shoulders because he can't talk. He has a sore throat. Then I cry because I don't want Grandpa to miss out on Love's visit. Love comes over and takes out a purple polka-dotted handkerchief, and wipes my eyes. Then he pulls out a pink hanky and a blue hanky and then a green one too. Love knows how to juggle, so he tries to juggle all of the handkerchiefs at once. Love can't juggle very good and they usually wind up in my lap or on my head. Then I laugh and laugh.

I laugh so hard that Nana comes out of the garage to see what is going on. Love acts so funny when he sees Nana! He holds his heart, bats his eyelashes, and swoons. Love goes over to the old Victorola and puts on the dancing music. We all dance and shake and twist and turn until Nana and Love and I all fall in a big heap on the floor.

I get up first so that I can help Nana back on her feet again. By the time Nana gets up, Love is gone. Nana and I look everywhere for him. We look in the boxes of Christmas decorations and behind the tall refrigerator boxes where Nana keeps the summer clothes. We search in the corner where Mommy's old baby pictures hang, and we look behind the water heater. Love has disappeared and that makes us very sad. Nana and I start to cry. When we stop crying, we go outside and see a rainbow! The rainbow holds onto the tree tops while it climbs and grows all the way up to heaven.

The warm sunshine comes out, and I splash in the puddles while Nana inspects her flowers. After a while, we go inside to find Grandpa sitting in the rocking chair reading the mail. " Here's a letter for you, my pretty," says Grandpa. I tear open the letter . Inside is a red heart cut out of construction paper. Grandpa helps me to read the big words that say" Dearest Lizzie, I know that you were unhappy when I left today, but don't you worry, I'll be back on another rainy day. When I leave you next time, you just come outside and wave to me when I dance up the rainbow to heaven. When I'm in heaven, I'll watch after you and make sure that you're happy.''

That side of the paper heart is all filled up, so I flip it over. On this side, I can read the words all by myself, ''I Love You, Lizzie! Your Friend, Love.''

POPAGALLO

by Victoria Stirling, *Salt Lake City, Utah*

About two years ago my Mom brought home a new pet. She said that it was an Amazon parrot. It had emerald green feathers on its body and on the top of his head he had light blue feathers. There were bright red feathers surrounding his beak with a little bit of yellow under his eyes; he looked like he was ready to go into battle with his war paint on. I didn't know what to think. We had a cockateel once, but all it did was screech and snap at us. After we had it a while, my Uncle came over and saw our new bird. He told us to give it the Spanish name for parrot and so we named him "Popagallo."

Now, Popagallo and I are just like best friends. Often I place him on my shoulder and walk around the house with him, like a pirate. Late at night, when he's tired, I will lie down on the sofa and put his back on my stomach. I hold his feet, so he feels secure, then I rub his stomach. Sometimes it even sounds like he's purring, like a cat! I can walk up to Popagallo almost any time and pet his head. He loves it if I scratch his neck and he feels smooth and velvety.

I have always thought that our parrot was really friendly, but my younger brothers don't agree. I guess that Popagallo likes me more than them (who can blame him), or maybe I just love him more than anyone else. When we first got Popagallo, the owners who had him before us taught him to say the usual, "Polly want a cracker," and "pretty birdie." However, after a little work and reforming, we gave him a new vocabulary. Whenever the telephone rings Popagallo shouts out, "Hello!" Once one of our neighbors knocked on the door and he shouted, "Come in!" They opened the door and no one was home except our parrot telling them to come inside. Now he has learned to say my name. Every day, right before school is over, he starts yelling, "Tory come here! Tory come here!" If no one picks him up he walks around the house looking for someone. If you call his name from another room, sometimes he will jump off his cage. You can hear his little claws tapping on the kitchen linoleum as he walks around looking for you.

Popagallo is one of the best pets I have ever had. I love to watch him playing around in his cage or grooming his beautiful feathers. We always have lots of fun together, either playing Super Bird as I run around the house with him, or giving him a bath. It's too bad that we can't trade in little brothers for a parrot!

THE BEST KIND OF LOVE
by Jonathan Tait, *New Bern, North Carolina*

My first girlfriend was in love with
me, in love with my money.

My second girlfriend was in love
with me, or should I say with my
older brother.

My third girlfriend was in love with
me for me, which is the best kind of
love for me.

She meant a lot to me.

One day, a truly dark one, she was hit by
a speeding car, the driver never looked
back.

I'm sure going to miss Magic, my pet
Cocker Spaniel.

WHAT IS IT LIKE
by Chi-Chu Tschang, *Fresno, California*

What is it like
to be in love
I think I used to love my old bike
But now it's in the big bike shop up above
Obviously, a girl and a bike are not quite alike.

Where do you draw the line
Do you have to be friends to be lovers
Or can it be a blind date you take to wine and dine
Is there really love at first sight or under covers
Or are you just lusting because she's sooooooo fine

Will I know when Cupid hits me with an arrow
Will I start to act like a fool
and my vision becomes so narrow
that the only thing I see is her at home, work, or school
Will my mind rot and start to fallow

Will I be filled with joy
Will I be filled with happiness and ecstacy
like a child with a new toy
like an Englishman with a spot of tea
Is it the same as witnessing the birth of your baby boy

How do I find this joy from a girl
Where should I even begin to look
Should I let it come to me and just stand still
Is all this information in some sort of book
If so, just point to the bookstore, if you will

More importantly, please tell me, Paul
why is love so confusing
Why can't it be simple like basketball
Is love some cruel joke that God finds so amusing
Or is it really his greatest gift of all

REBIRTH

by Jaci Miller, *Osceola, Indiana*

Myself, a word I cannot bear,
resentful, painful, with despair;
mockery, injustice, without good cause
bring silent teardrops without pause.
Yet no one sees this soundless rain
so torture continues; doubles the pain.

The hurt's gone on for many years
never ceasing for pleas or tears
so myself, I do dislike,
and through my heart there is a spike.
One day the sun will break the rain and
take my sorrow, take my pain.
The word myself shall be again
the word that means, I am my friend.

My family, faith and caring friends,
gave me courage to make amends.
To trust in me and make the best
and to keep me high on my own friend list.

The world had taken my self-worth
but now I know I love me,
so this is my rebirth.

REFLECTIONS OF A SUBVERSIVE ROMANTIC

by Chris Flink, *Aurora, Colorado*

I'm not the best guy to ask about love. Any of the natural, dewy innocence in me was quashed by the process of watching my mother through two divorces. The little mediocre poet who lurks in the clavicles of us all has been gassed in me by the fumes of cynicism that have by this point so permeated my own lungs that the very words I speak (and write — I guess some's been concentrated in my hands too) are suffused with those selfsame noxious emanations. Therefore, ever since I ended my early emulation of a sometimes namesake, Mr. Edgar Allen Poe, I have not been able to flog that little Robert Blyish figure swimming in his own putrid self-obsessed, self-absorbed, (which he'd damn well better be, to wipe up what he spews out) navel-gazing into helping me put onto paper any bad love poetry.

To be honest, I've spent as much time as any self-respecting teenage angst-volcano writing, instead of long dissertations about my latest lady (or whatever) love, bathetically out of reach, pseudo-deep ruminations on my own perceived inadequacies and failures (as opposed to my failings). However, though I recognize my activities as perhaps more pretentious and adducially literary, they were darned heartfelt. Doesn't that count for something? Actually, I think nothing counts more, so I can't muster any true contempt for those who are in love and describe what they feel honestly and with some humor. Which leaves all the more bile for self-mythologizing twits who project their carefully nurtured, canned emotions into ideas and statements of significance. You see, love is pretty common, and if I have to experience it vicariously, (more on this later) I'd rather do so with someone who portrays the sweetness and gentle surrealism of something that derives its transcendence precisely from its mundanity.

I'm bored with love. I can't listen to music without hearing about it. I can't watch the tube without being bombarded by it — mostly during commercial breaks. Breathy teens (more or less like me) use the damn word obsessively, in a last desperate attempt to escape the utter triviality of their suburban existences (more or less like mine) by convincing themselves that they are part of that which makes the world go 'round, that which inane people ever since Eustacia Vye have sought, in hopes that it'll make everything all right. Well, it won't. God, I hate love.

Author's Note: This was written in a sitting. The time doesn't matter, but the setting does; I'm in a great mood. You see, for the first time in what has seemed an arctic eternity, I am taken. A longtime friend, always up for a fight over something stupid, and I have taken up with each other. I have been taken up in the arms of the Goddess of Love; I am being swung through arcs of nirvanic ecstasy, on my way to heaven by way of cloud nine. And I think it's really nice. This probably does nasty things to my thesis, but, then again, would I be telling you this if I really minded?

EJIDO TLAXCALA: LEARNING TO LOVE

by Cindy Blackwell, *Aurora, CO*

O n the airplane hundreds of thoughts careened through my mind. I wondered how a tiny Mexican village was going to react to a group of twenty-five gringos. I thought that if I were one of the natives I wouldn't welcome a group of outsiders who wanted to replace my religion with theirs. Maybe what we're doing isn't right, I think. Maybe they should be left alone, to believe what they want to believe. I was nervous about the trip and about how different this week in the tiny border town of Tlaxcala would be for an average American girl from the suburbs.

When we arrived at camp it was dark and all the other tents were already in place. With difficulty we assembled our tents, went to chapel, and retired for the night. We were told that our first day in the village would be long and to get plenty of rest. Unfortunately, there was too much adrenaline pumping through all of our bodies for anyone to sleep well. In the hazy light of morning we groggily rose and made our way to breakfast and then to chapel. Sitting in the dirt during the chapel service would become natural before the week was completed. We prayed as a team before we left that the village would welcome us and that our love would be clear. However, I was not expecting to be welcomed.

As we drove down the dusty dirt road, I looked out the window, and all that I could focus on was the obvious poverty of the region. There were tattered clothes blowing on make-shift clotheslines and rusted out trucks abandoned on the sides of the road. Each corner had dingy little stores that advertised with Spanish Coca-Cola signs.

Finally we pulled into Ejido Tlaxcala. It was typical of the border towns that I had already seen. No paved streets, no multi-room houses, and farm animals meandered care-lessly around town. I had prepared myself for the impover-ished people, and I was ready to deal with the dirt and the sweat. What I was not ready for was the love that these peo-ple, who had nothing, lavished on those of us who thought we had everything. From the minute we stepped out of our vans each morning, through the Vacation Bible School pro-gram, during our lunch time, through the "siesta" hours of the afternoon, and until we closed the van doors to return to camp, the people of Tlaxcala shared with us. I was hugged and kissed by what seemed like thousands of children with jet black hair and deep brown eyes, but in real-ity was only a few whose capacity for loving was greater than I had ever known was possible.

I had decided to go on this trip to Mexico because I had thought that it would be a chance for me to help out some poor people. I figured that I should share some of my good fortune with those who didn't have the privileges and op-portunities that I had learned to take for granted. As I look back, I know that the week I spent in Tlaxcala, working, teaching, and being dirty, showed me how poor I was. How odd, that a few small children who live in one room houses with dirt floors taught me more about love in one week than I have learned from anyone or anything else in the rest of my seventeen years.

WE JOURNEYED TOGETHER
by Thomas B. Campbell, IV, *Pensacola, Florida*

I met you when I was but a little child,
almost unknown to the world around me,
unknowing of that same world of vastness,
its ability to simply swallow something up,
never to be seen again.
Our life was not a bad life,
growing up together without a care in the world.

Later on, we would grow extremely weary
of each other at times,
as the closest of friends always will.
You asked me once, "Do you even care about me?"
I could only say, "My love is the only proof."
I then found
your love was 180 proof.
We didn't talk much after that,
growing only further and further apart.

You moved away for a time, how long, I don't know.
I made myself too busy to try to see you,
too busy even to care, and you became but a hidden
    memory.
Then came the time you were coming back, and I was
    scared,

scared not of you, not even of your problem.
Knowing with your inner strength, it was a problem no
    longer,
but scared of my feelings for you,
scared of wanting to see you again after all you had
    done to me,
scared of your feelings for me.
Seeing you brought back those memories, so carefully
    hidden,
memories of our childhood together, and of yours,
    hidden from me until now.
It brought back the bad, which I had tried never to
    remember,
but also the good, which I had tried never to forget.
We had become friends once again.

While we journeyed together down the roads of life,
You took one of the paths least taken, overrun with
    thorns and bushes,
and I was alone.
Now, you have come out okay and are reaching the end
    of your journey.
I'm trying to pull you into mine, as our paths separate,
and I think it's working.

Together down the road, it's a longer journey than
    either of us thought,

Thomas B. Campbell, IV

Sometimes seemingly never ending.
Together down that never ending path we go.

And as I answer your question once again,
I love you, Mom.

THE YIN AND YANG OF MING SHAN

by Michele Ming Shan Smith, *Makakilo, HI*

My boyfriend and I have nicknames for each other — he's Yang, I'm Yin. I used to think that the elements of two people were needed to complete the circle, but now I realize that my own personality contains the qualities of both Yin and Yang.

"Yin—Shady; secret; dark. Mysterious. Cold. The negative or female principle in nature; it is the opposite of Yang."

Yang—Clear; bright. The sun. Heat. Pertaining to this world. Superior. Upper. Front."

—Matthew's Chinese Dictionary

In spite of the fact that Yang is "upper, "Yin is the dominant half of my personality. I am often quiet and reflective, for Yin keeps her own counsel. Even when in a large crowd, I may seem only "half there." All is hidden behind the screen of Chinese inscrutability.

To be Yin is to look inside one's self. Introspective and watchful, she shies away from human contact, holding back because she is afraid of getting hurt. She confuses others to avoid exposing her true self. Like a dark attic, she is the keeper of many secrets. Something special is often discovered by the clear beam of a flashlight accidentally illuminating a long-forgotten corner.

Like the typical Chinese wife, Yin is timid and soft spoken. She is afraid to express herself and can't easily articulate her feelings. Yin is the pale golden moon on a cloudy, windy night. Always hiding, always running. She is the heartbeat of a shadow in the dark.

While Yin is a naive and innocent maiden, Yang is a cocksure young god. He stands up and takes charge. He knows he is the best. When Yang speaks, people listen. He is always wise and right. Yang is in love with life and living.

He often shocks Yin by the bold and daring feats he performs for her entertainment. She smiles timorously while he laughs ingratiatingly. Yang is friendly and gregarious, looking at the world with fresh, unjaded eyes. While Yin is daydreaming and writing poetry in her room, Yang is shaking hands and campaigning for office in the front yard.

Yang is haole, a foreigner. He is an engaging invader into Yin's world. She is constantly amused and entertained by his antics, yet disturbed that she likes him so much.

Yang loves Yin for her gentle voices and soft vulnerability; he knows she needs him. Yin loves Yang because he is strong and invincible, yet she knows he needs her, too. They thoroughly enjoy each other's company, but often don't understand each other. Yin and Yang are total and complete opposites; because of this, they work well together.

Yang is the brightness of the rising sun. He is the eternal optimist because he knows everything will be okay in the end. Yang is omnipotent. What he says, goes. He does not force people to his will, but they come around anyway. They just can't help it because they like him so much.

Yang is the naked, boastful splendor of sunset. Yin is the lightly falling hand of dusk. Where Yang goes, Yin follows. It is said that behind every successful man there is a supportive woman. Behind every Yang is a Yin.

THE BOND

by Skip Travers, *New Bern, North Carolina*

I love the game of baseball. However, there is more to the game than the game itself.

The love I feel for the bonding and camaraderie experienced between the players is a stronger, more intense, overwhelming love than I have ever felt. The love creates itself during the obstacles we face together during the season. I feel along with my teammates the intoxicating thrill of victory. We endure the desolation and misery of defeat. Together we develop a protective relationship which ties us to one another.

The connection between us players feels its greatest after a victory. All mistakes are briefly forgotten, winners take all. The players unite, the celebration begins. Big plays become bigger; balls are hit farther; pitches become faster. We glorify the game amongst ourselves. A fleeting feeling of harmony and pure bliss becomes mutual between the team.

Although, it is in defeat the bond really emerges and is created. A strong team crippled by a loss cannot survive alone, but must turn to each other for support. The connection arises from the common realization that as players we failed and only as a team we can overcome and triumph. There will always be the hope that tomorrow, together we will prevail.

The link displays itself to its greatest visibility and

magnitude when fellow players are challenged, The protective relationship holds true to belief of "taking care of your own." Even the most detested player will become as close as a brother when threatened by a person foreign to the team. The strong bond is never verbally mentioned, but understood and silently spoken by our actions.

In the end, the connection created among the team while playing baseball directly translates to the relationships created during life. Obtaining success in life cannot be accomplished alone. Individually we are destined to collapse. Only with our team, whether it may be family, friends, or co-workers, will we accomplish our goal.

The quiet bond developed is called love.

IF

by **Sharon Fuller,** *Houston, Texas*

If I run away from you
will you find me
When I cry "I hate you"
Will you say "I love you" I mean
if I push will you hold me till
I stop and fall in your arms?
Will you?

LOVE
by Jodie Turner, *Dallas, Texas*